GLADIATOR DOGS

BY
DR. CARL SEMENCIC

los angeles

The author wishes to acknowlege the wonderful photographers who contributed their work for this book. Special thanks to Markus Rogen and Hyungwon Kang, for their generosity and superior photography. The following individuals provided photos for this book: Serena Burnett, Barbara and Manuel Curto, Gina Brischi Douglas, Isabelle Francais, Mitchell Photography, Rafael Tejada, Marianne Walz, Malcolm Wren, and Redmond Young—and anyone we have inadvertently omitted!

This book is a reissue of the original edition, with new layout.

Published in the USA by
Digital Fabulists
11684 Ventura Blvd #205
Studio City, CA 91604
www.digitalfabulists.com

ISBN-10: 0615850243
ISBN-13: 978-0615850245

Cover photo: Sigi Aler's Canary bitch, named Jessy.
Title page opposite: Canary Dog owned by Manuel Curto.

Printed in the United States of America

In Memory of Jan Bracke, Canary Dog Breeder
and "all–around good guy"

Table of Contents

Preface to the Latest Release of *Gladiator Dogs*

My third book about dogs, entitled *Gladiator Dogs*, was published in 1998. It was doing very well when the publishing house that published it was sold and the new publisher decided to disassociate itself from all three of my books, probably because of the nature of the subject matter of these books. To be honest, a great number of copies had sold already at that point and I was neither here or there on the matter of selling more books going forward but for two problems. One was that I hadn't seen the sale of my publisher and the discontinuation of my books coming so I hadn't bought a few copies for myself!

The second problem that for years people were writing me, emailing me or calling me asking me where they could get a copy of *Gladiator Dogs* and I, not having even a few copies for myself, couldn't help them.

Years went by and those who had stocked up on copies of *Gladiator Dogs* were selling them for as much as $600. each! As I am sitting here right now, there is a "new" copy being offered on amazon.com for $496.01 plus $3.99 for shipping. One day a novelist I know put me in touch with her publisher, he and I had a conversation and he offered to republish the book at his expense. I had nothing to lose. The rights to the book had reverted to me when the publisher dropped the title and if the publisher was going to do the job for free, my only investment would be the time it would take to correct a few errors the first publisher had made and correct any errors the new publisher would make in transcribing the manuscript. These were minor. For example, anywhere in the original book that I used the word "modern," the new publisher changed the word to "modem." I don't know why but it was easily correctable.

So here I am, fifteen years after the publication of *Gladiator Dogs,* writing an introduction to the new release of the book. Fifteen years ago I would have bet you a thousand dollars that this day would never come but I'd have lost that bet because here it is so as long as we are here, let's talk about the book a bit.

My dog books were a unique experience for me. They put me in contact with all manner of people from all over the world and in many instances I really enjoyed the acquaintances I made. Some were doctors, many lawyers, some veterinarians, many police officers of various rank, etc.

and it is always enjoyable to chat about a favorite interest with intelligent people. On the other side of the coin, when talking about tough dogs you are also going to get second hand criticism from the peanut gallery. People who live in what I consider to be squalor with little more than a pot to … whatever in and who have nothing to boost their egos with other than that some other idiot agrees with him or her when he or she declares my books to be full of inaccuracies, etc. These people were always meaningless to me because in their lives they never contributed anything to the overall body of knowledge, are not contributing anything and will never contribute anything. Their greatest glory will be to criticize me for being who they wish they were. Sad.

The breeds discussed in this book have come a long way since I began writing dog books. For example, the Dogue de Bordeaux was well on its way to extinction when I had an article published in *Dog World Magazine* on the breed called "Introducing the Dogue de Bordeaux." At the time there were 600 individual examples of the breed in the world, none in the United States and the numbers were on the decline. Today they are registered with the American Kennel Club where they are listed in the "Working Group" and their use is described as "Guardian; Hunter." Give me a break A.K.C.! Don't these people know anything about dogs?

One of my greatest regrets is that back when, I thought I had more time to introduce the Doquin de Bordeaux to the world outside of France. I put that introduction on the back burner until my introduction of the Dogue was complete and by the time I got around to going back to France to take a few pictures of Doquins, they had gone extinct. THAT is how fragile the condition of some of these breeds were when I began to write about them.

Incidentally, I have heard more than once that it was the movie "Turner and Hooch" that was responsible for the introduction of the Dogue de Bordeaux breed to the United States. False. That movie didn't come out until 1989 (search it on the web) and the dogs used were obtained from a guy who learned about the breed from me. My article in *Dog World* came out in 1982 and my first book, *The World of Fighting Dogs*, which dedicated a chapter to the Dogue, was published in 1984. So, sorry breed historians who would like to re-write the history of this breed but it was me who saved the breed and while you can deny it, anyone interested in learning the truth can prove you wrong very easily.

But that's the way it's been with the work I've done to bring little known breeds to public attention. So many want to re-write history and give the credit to anyone but me, regardless of the very easily provable facts. Is it frustrating? At times, but it is what it is and the truth is what it is and anyone who matters to me knows that. Furthermore, I am confident that politically correct dog registry organizations not withstanding, my day will come and everyone will have to recognize who did what and when.

In any event, it will be interesting to see how this book does once it is released again. I'm sure there will be those who will write negative reviews of the book either because they haven't read it, they always wanted to be the big rare breed expert themselves and couldn't be, etc. But as for you, reader, I hope you will enjoy the book, remember to view it within its historical context and think of me whenever someone offers some false history of the breeds discussed here.

Salute!

Canary Dog owned by Manuel Curto.

Acknowledgments

It is absolutely impossible for me to acknowledge the many friends, acquaintances, and correspondents who played a role in the production of this book. So many people have sent me photographs over the years, some of which have been used here and some of which have not. So many people have written to simply "talk dogs" and to pass on what they have heard about and what they have done with dogs. And so many people have either written, or otherwise gotten in contact with me, simply to offer the occasional word of encouragement. These words of encouragement were more valuable than these people might realize. After all, writing a dog book is meant to be fun, and without these words of encouragement the project would not have been fun, and so I would not have embarked upon it.

But as it is not possible to name everyone who should be named, I will name only a few who immediately come to mind, in no particular order. There is Dept. Chief Gerry Pleasant, who as busy as he is chasing bad guys, never fails to put time aside to give me a call and chat dogs. There is Markus Rogen of Germany, a professional photographer and veterinarian who sent me zillions of fantastic photographs for use in my book out of the goodness of his heart. There is Hyungwon Kang, staff photographer with the *L.A. Times* who not only was anxious to pass on information on the Korean Jindo breed, a breed of which he is especially proud, and fantastic photographs of these rare dogs, but who then produced a beautiful, pure white, Jindo puppy that he has graciously offered to send me as a gift!

There's my old buddy, Eddie Dombish, a dog trainer from New York City, who is always there and ready to launch himself into some tirade of opinion about this breed or that. There's Todd Fenstermacher and Aaron Dial, two knowledgeable students of rare purebreds and of purebred history with whom I have chatted dogs "ad naseum."

And there's my family, Barbara, Alex and Dan, who really couldn't care less about these dogs but who are in a position in which they have no choice but to make the best of them as a result of being stuck with me.

Thanks for everything family and friends. I'll start talking about something else now.

Korean Jindo puppy photographed by Hyungwon Kang.

The author's mother, Frances Semencic,
with her Bulldog "Petey" (photographed
in Brooklyn, circa 1920).

Dedication

This book is dedicated to my parents, the late Frances Semencic (Maria Francesca Favorito) and the late Antun Semencic (Tony). Sometimes I wonder how I became interested in these strange dogs, and yet, as I think back to the family stories I grew up with, I recall my father having spoken repeatedly of the Bull Terrier that he and his crew kept on one of the ships he sailed on for a long time, and a "Japanese Fighting Dog" (when I showed him a picture of a Tosa once he said, "Yeah. That's it") that he sailed with on another ship. My Mom had a million stories about her family dog, "Petey," a big white American Bulldog that she grew up with. I guess you never know what's rubbing off.

These two didn't have a lot to give me in the way of money, but they taught me how to survive in this world of ours, and I'll never forget them for it. I hope I'm doing as good a job at passing this lesson on.

A Note to the Reader

Before you begin looking through this book, there are a couple of things I would like to say that I think are important. I hope you'll bear with me here for just a minute.

I've tried to assemble some good and, in some cases, rare photographs for use in this book. I've also taken care to write a caption for each photograph that is relevant to that which I have tried to communicate to you by using the photograph. I intend the photographs to be educational and I intend to try to write informative captions as well. But in spite of its numerous pictures, I do not mean this to be a "picture book." This is a book of chapters as well, and it is in the writing that is contained in these chapters in which I put forth the bulk of the information that I want to present to you about these breeds.

If it is information about these dogs that you purchased this book for, reading the chapters will be required. It will not be sufficient to look at the pictures and to read the captions. If you do not read the chapters, you will not know what my opinion of this or that is. You will not know what information I have uncovered about this or that. The real meat of this book is in the chapters—not only in the breed chapters, but in all the chapters. This is a book that was written to be read.

Also, this is a book about breeds of dogs that were bred for the sport of dogfighting. The fact that many breeds were originally bred for dogfighting purposes and that some breeds are still bred for dogfighting purposes is a reality—like it or not. The fact that the sport of dogfighting has been a pastime among so many people of the world for thousands of years and that it remains a sport that is actively participated in today by people all over the globe is also an indisputable reality. This is a book that confronts and explains this reality. It is not a book that condones or promotes dogfighting as a sport.

On occasion I will find myself in a position in which I have to suffer through someone's criticism of something I have said in my book, only to realize as the person is complaining that he or she has not read the book but is reacting to some erroneous conclusion drawn as a result of scanning the pictures or the chapter headings or as a result of someone else's hearsay. This can be frustrating because it is a waste of time. But worse than this is the accusation that anyone who brings the world of dogfighting out into the open, as I have, is condoning dogfighting or, perhaps, is a dog fighter himself. This goes beyond being frustrating. This makes me angry. It makes me angry not only on a personal level, but more importantly because this attitude that speech should be suppressed is a dangerous one. It isn't something that should be part of our society. It's beneath us as intelligent people. Just imagine what would happen if we adopted this attitude toward all crimes and other matters that we found distasteful.

So read the book, now that you have bought it. Perhaps one has to be very involved in a particular breed discussed here in order to appreciate how controversial some of the information offered sometimes is, but even if you are just a casual reader and purebred enthusiast I think you will find the information contained here to be the beginning of a good, no nonsense, straightforward education on the subject of these dogs and their place in human history.

German Champion Spice, one of the gamest stud dogs in Germany. Spice was confiscated by police and deported to a shelter. The dog is said to have been stolen from the shelter, and when its owner was acquitted of the charge of dogfighting, Spice couldn't be found!

Introduction

From my perspective, it seems the entire world has changed since I wrote my first book *The World of Fighting Dogs* in 1984. So many changes have occurred in my life, throughout the country, throughout the world and, more relevant to this book, in the world of dogs, that it's hard to imagine that in the overall scheme of things, so little time has passed.

One major change that has taken place, again, purely from my perspective, is that the Pit Bull Terrier I dedicated that first book to is long since gone. Nugget was just shy of his 14th birthday when the time came for him to cash in his chips. He had been with me since his puppyhood and when the time came for me to do the merciful thing and have him

Bill Hines's Georgia Gal, a working 70-pound bitch
at 14 months of age, is from a very good strain of
hogdogs out of northeastern Georgia.

put down, I did what I had to do. Although he's been gone for well over a decade now, I still keep a picture of him and me together, prominently displayed on my desk, so that I can look at it every day. Oddly, I've had other dogs since, but for whatever reason, it's Nugget's picture that sits on my desk.

When I first got Nugget I was a single college student, using my parents' apartment in Queens, New York City, as my home base. By the time Nugget died, I had a Ph.D., I owned a home, I was married and my first son had already been born. Now both of my parents are gone and where once there were two parents, there are now two sons, Alexander and Daniel. Two Semencics gone and two born. Who was it who said, "The more things change, the more they stay the same?"

Nationally and internationally things have changed too. We could argue about whether the condition of our country is better or worse now than it was when *The World of Fighting Dogs* first hit the shelves, but I have that argument often enough as it is. Suffice it to say that things are quite different than they were, like it or not. Things are pretty different in the communist world too, I dare say.

But this isn't a book about me, or about either national or international politics. It is a book about dogs and within this subject, it is a book about "the gladiator breeds." With regard to these dogs, the world has changed very dramatically too.

Consider the breeds I talked about in *The World of Fighting Dogs*. The American Pit Bull Terrier had just begun to develop a reputation as a dangerous dog back then. The average person didn't know what a Pit Bull was and among those who knew the breed minimally, most were more inclined to

That's your smiling author, with a fine, steady black Tosa that was on display at a large Pet Expo not far from his home. That's Tosa breeder Steve Ostuni looking on.

associate these dogs with Petey of the "Our Gang" comedy series than with dog fights or with attacks upon people. Now the very breed name "Pit Bull" is synonymous with unbridled aggression and not only does the average person think he knows what a Pit Bull is but, in some areas of the country, legislation has been proposed and, in some instances, passed to outlaw these dogs. We'll talk more about how this change came about in the appropriate chapter. For now, suffice it to say that the Pit Bull breed is much more widely recognized now than it was in 1984.

Consider the American Bulldog, the Tosa, and the Dogue de Bordeaux. When I sat down to write my first book, these dogs were virtually unknown in this country. In the case of the Dogue de Bordeaux, when I first discovered this breed and began to write about it, Bordeaux Dogues were very rare in Europe, even in their native France, and were all but non existent in the United States. The American Bulldog was totally unknown outside of the United States and was virtually unknown in the United States. We might even speculate that the American Bulldog was on the brink of extinction when I began to write that first book. The Tosa was seen by the few Americans who had heard of it as more myth than reality and even in Japan, many dog fighters were giving up their Tosas in favor of the often gamer, always smaller, and easier to feed American Pit Bull Terrier. Few Japanese were working at perfecting a typical Tosa body style and certainly no dog breeders outside of Japan were worried about the preservation of this breed.

Now the major purebred dog magazines are literally overloaded with ads for the Bordeaux Dogue, the American Bulldog and to some extent the Tosa. Especially in the case

The author is pleased to be presenting many great dogs from around this world, like this fine Dogue de Bordeaux from Germany.

of the American Bulldog I am forever hearing that there are far more dogs and far more people breeding these dogs than the puppy market can possibly bear. Initially prices for puppies skyrocketed, first doubling, then tripling and finally becoming five, six and seven times what they had been when I first began to talk to the few breeders who had these dogs about what a good pup would cost. Now they have begun to come down because as in demand as these dogs are, there are enough breeders willing to sell puppies for reasonable prices so that prospective buyers are in a position to say "No" to the outrageous prices that were being charged so recently.

How about the Olde Bulldogge, as recreated by Dave Leavitt, and the Bandog, as originally recreated by John Swinford? How did all of the notoriety of being discussed in that first book change the future of these dogs? Or, on the opposite end of the popularity spectrum, the Akita and the Shar-Pei. These breeds were already exploding in popularity when my first book was published. We'll talk about how the situation has changed since 1984 for these dogs as well.

It is because so much has changed since the publication of *The World of Fighting Dogs* that I decided I should write this book as a "follow up." This is my third book on dogs, but the second book, *Pit Bulls & Tenacious Guard Dogs,* was never intended to be at all like the first book. This book will be much like the first book, up to date, and with much more detail added. The reasons that more detail will be offered here are that there is simply more detail available now than there was prior to 1984 as a result of there being so many more of these dogs now than there were prior to 1984 and because with so many people involved in these dogs now, each bringing his or her own ideas to each breed and so influencing the direction of the breed in question. I feel it is time to step back, look at the history of each breed again, and allow the history to offer the direction that so many are searching for and arguing over.

Of Politics
and Fighting Dogs

I have never been a big fan of "laws," and I am especially opposed to the establishment of an abundance of laws. Society obviously needs to establish laws in order to keep itself in check. I am by no means an anarchist, but rather more of a libertarian with regard to my willingness to allow others to establish laws by which I must abide. As such, my general philosophy, as it regards laws and law making, is that we should establish as few laws as are necessary to protect ourselves from our fellow man (and to keep ourselves traveling along the straight and narrow), and we should make it our business to enforce the few laws that we do establish in no uncertain terms in order that our laws will remain meaningful.

A rare photograph depicting a dogfight in progress
many years ago.

It has been my observation that society establishes far
more laws than it needs and even far more laws than make
any sense at all, for the simple reason that it fails to enforce
the few well-constructed laws that it already has. As a case
in point, consider the many proposed gun bans that our
society faces today. We have written what would seem to be
very effective laws regarding the purchase and use of guns.
Essentially, in their most "liberal" form, they are that an adult
American who has no criminal record may purchase and
own a gun, but that he or she may not commit crimes with
this gun. The constitution of the United States of America
tells us that this is our birthright, right?

Wrong. What happens the first time a 14-year-old
purchases a handgun illegally and uses this handgun while
committing a crime? Do we stand tall and declare that the
law of the land has been violated and that those responsible
for the commission of this series of serious crimes must pay?

No. Instead, the most powerful fighting force the world has ever known (you and me) rolls over on its belly with its tail between its legs and screams, "Uh. We're in trouble now! There's no way we can punish a 14-year-old and there's certainly no way that we can find out who provided this 14-year-old with a gun and prosecute that person. So let's throw the Constitution away and write a new law that states that no person can ever own a gun again." And what will our society do when that law is passed on a national level and even the average person begins to observe that now, only criminals have guns? It will write another law, and then another, and then another, until finally the law-abiding citizen can't walk down the street without getting himself arrested, while the lawless will continue to do as they please, as they have done all along.

A smiling two-year-old male Bull Terrier named
Arlekino Archie Caprisse, owned by Marina Belyava
of Russia.

3

This is Nikki, niece of Bordeaux Dogue breeder
Wendy Norris, with a young pup.

So what is it that makes me think that you, the reader of my book about dogs, could care less about my political philosophy as it regards the establishment of laws? Well, as most of you have undoubtedly already figured out, we live in a country, and in fact in a world, which now regards guns and the fighting breeds in precisely the same way. We have long since had good laws which direct us in the keeping of our dogs. We must own our dogs responsibly. We must prevent our dogs from doing harm to others. We must prevent our dogs from annoying others, within reason. It would seem that such laws would suffice, wouldn't it?

Apparently they do not suffice. Because the lawless ignore the law (by definition) and because society is incapable of dealing with the lawless in a manner that will reaffirm the strength of our laws (and so of our society), we write new laws and we campaign for the establishment of even more laws, in spite of the fact that these new laws are often redundant, at best, and more often, mindless. We bury ourselves in legislation, each generation of politicians opting for the short-term solution to the political pressures brought upon them by the citizenry screaming for the enforcement of laws, which is to say that each generation of politicians either proposes or backs further legislation aimed at dealing with simple societal problems in the hopes that by the time the public figures out that the new legislation is more useless than the old, they, themselves, will be retired or booted out of office anyway.

Today we live in an America in which many feel that society would be best served if the American Pit Bull

While England is the home base of the Bull Terrier, the breed has thrived in Germany for many years. This napping BT was bred by Rudolf Sewerin of Germany.

Terrier and other fighting breeds were made illegal. We live in a world in which many countries have already made the Pit Bull and other breeds, some of which are fighting breeds and some of which are not, totally illegal. I may be incapable of expressing to you just how sick, how self destructive, how "wimpish" it sounds to sit back and listen to a country fight to establish such laws for itself. Unlike many of you, I suppose, I have had the experience of doing precisely this.

Four years ago, I got a call from a television station in Birmingham, England, asking me if I would be willing to fly to England to debate members of Parliament, representatives from the RSPCA (the Royal Society for the Prevention of Cruelty to Animals), representatives of the police force, and others, on the subject of whether or not to totally ban the Pit Bull Terrier from the United Kingdom. The proposed legislation specified that no new Pit Bulls would be allowed into the United Kingdom and already existing Pit Bulls would be disallowed from producing puppies. Ownership of Pit Bulls would be completely banned if this legislation were to be passed.

As the television station was picking up the tab for both my wife and me to go to Birmingham and for us to stay at a good hotel while there, and as I was actually interested in doing my part to help the British protect themselves from themselves, I agreed to go. To this day I am not sorry I went. In retrospect, I am glad that I didn't know ahead of time what a witch hunt the television show was to be or I might have felt that the entire trip was not worthwhile.

To make a long story short (and I was on TV for about an hour, so it is a fairly long story), the entire studio audience of roughly 90 people was composed of English men and women who absolutely loathed Pit Bulls and wanted them totally banned from the United Kingdom. Only a handful of people present dared to question the need for further "dangerous dog" legislation when perfectly adequate legislation was already on the books which provided for penalties for those who kept their dogs in a manner that was dangerous to others. One "MP," or Member of Parliament, expressed this opinion and the reaction of the crowd was such that I would not be at all surprised to learn that he has since been booted out of office as a result of that evening's appearance.

The crowd was downright hostile to the idea that there was nothing inherently wrong with Pit Bulls, as a breed, or with any other breed, and that the problem was poor ownership and lack of enforcement of existing legislation when examples of poor ownership were discovered. Instead, they called for the passage of the legislation that was ultimately passed. Today, the Pit Bull Terrier, the Dogo Argentino (for some reason that I will never understand), the Fila Brasiliero, and other dogs, are completely illegal in England.

I must confess that although both my wife Barbara and I had a great time in the English countryside, and although I got to see the birthplace of the immortal bard, William Shakespeare, on a beautiful spring day, I found myself uncontrollably humming "God Bless America" all the way home. As a result, I did not surprise myself when, one year exactly to the date that I had been flown to Birmingham, I received a call from the same TV station asking me if I'd be willing to fly back to England to discuss a possible banning of the Tosa dog. This time, realizing what I would be in for if I made the trip, I declined the offer to go and make a personal appearance, but I accepted their offer to be satellite

Photographer and veterinarian Markus Rogen with
Tough Guy's Baby, a protection dog that can destroy
the arm guard of an attack suit with one bite (the
same arm guards that can last ten years with
a German Shepherd).

beamed from a television station on Manhattan's Upper West
Side to Birmingham in order to participate in the debate.
(Modern technology is incredible, isn't it?)

As I had suspected, it was the same witch hunt that it had
been the time before. I did my best. The owners of the only
Tosa in the United Kingdom did their best to defend their
breed as well. But in the end, the outcome was the same. In
addition to the Pit Bull, the Fila and the Dogo, the Tosa is
also banned in England.

But it isn't only the British who have instituted breed-
specific legislation. Many countries throughout Europe and
throughout the world have banned Pit Bulls in spite of all
of the evidence which clearly indicates that the Pit Bull
problem is a problem of poor ownership that could affect

many breeds and not a problem that is inherent to Pit Bulls specifically. Today, many Americans feel that the simplest solution to the perceived "Pit Bull problem" is to ban Pit Bulls, as has been done elsewhere. They forget the old story of the man who says that "when they came for this group, I didn't care because I wasn't a member of this group. When they came for that group I didn't care because I wasn't a member of that group either. But when they came for me, I was powerless, because they had already taken everyone else."

It is unlikely that I will ever be in a position again to suggest to you that we, as a people, be much more careful than we have been in the past and than we are being now, in appointing lawmakers to office who make laws that will benefit nothing but their own careers. As such, let me take this one opportunity to do so now. It would seem so ridiculous that we have reached a point at which we are passing laws against the ownership of the family dog. But this is precisely what we are doing. The Pit Bull is no more dangerous than its owner makes it. If it is inherently dangerous, compared to an inanimate object for example, then many other breeds of dogs are as well, and, as such, legislation which will govern the ownership of Pit Bulls should apply to the ownership of all dogs and not be aimed at the Pit Bull and related breeds. The Pit Bull has been among us for many generations. If they are an inherently dangerous breed, why is it only now that this dangerous trait has been discovered? Such questions need to be asked and then answered in a rational manner before even more inane legislation is added to the books to govern the way you and I will live our lives.

While we chew the fat, this Pit Bull pup will chew his
newly won trophy.

Let's Play
Question and Answer

I am amazed at the number of letters that I have received over the years from people who have read one or both of my books, have had a question about one thing or another, and have taken the initiative to sit themselves down and write me a letter. I am especially appreciative, by the way, of those who have seen fit to include a self-addressed stamped envelope with their letter to me. I guess writing letters to people who have written articles or books is the kind of thing I have done in the past myself, but it never occurred to me that so many others are so much like me in this regard.

I've enjoyed reading, and in many instances responding, to those letters. Before going on here, let me preface all of this by apologizing to those who have written letters I have not responded to. My failure to respond to your letter should not be construed to mean that I was uninterested in what you had to say or in your question. My reasons for not responding tend to fall in one of three categories.

First, there are times I am just too busy, either working or trying to write something else, to respond immediately and sometimes, by the time I get around to responding, the question to me is so old that it doesn't make sense to respond to it anymore. Second, mail is generally sent to my publisher. The publisher will sometimes let the mail sit around until they have a package of mail to send me and then forward it to me. By the time I get the mail some of it is very old and if I happen to be busy when the package comes, the sheer amount of mail requiring a response overwhelms me and I ignore it after having read it.

But my third reason for not responding to mail is the most relevant to this book. It is that while over the years I have gotten a great deal of mail from a number of people in every area of the world, many of the questions are the same questions over and over again. Some of these questions are good ones, and some are not so good. Regardless of the quality of the question, however, there are only so many times that a person can respond to the same question before one can't face the question anymore. It actually occurred to me once to simply print up a stock answer and mail it out in response to the questions that tend to be asked often, but this struck me as being even more impersonal than not responding at all, and perhaps even offensive.

A good-looking Pit Bull from Germany.

In any event, I hope those who have written to me with what must have seemed like friendly enough innocent questions will excuse me if you are among those who did not get a response. By way of response I thought I would try to answer a few of the questions that I have gotten repeatedly here. Perhaps these questions and answers will be of interest to others as well.

Q: You said in your first book that you did not want to rank the fighting breeds with regard to their fighting ability because you felt that all of these breeds should be positioned on a pedestal together. My question is, how would you rank the fighting breeds with regard to their fighting ability?

A: This question was very recently asked by Paul Egger of NSW, Australia, but this very day it came to me again via the Internet from one Darrin King who asks the question in the following form: Speaking of the fighting breeds, Darrin writes, "In my experience, they are the most reliable, loyal, and athletic dogs in existence. This said, however, I am still very interested in something you left out of your first book for reasons I understand. I would like to know the rough rank ordering pit men have observed in the fighting breeds. Would you consider relating this information?"

I have to admit that there are three answers to this incredibly common question. One answer is rude but from the heart. The next answer is philosophical. The third answer is academic. First the rude: What did I just say? I said I didn't want to rank the fighting breeds with regard to their fighting ability. What part of "I don't want to" didn't you understand? Next, the seriously philosophical: What's the difference? For your purposes these are all great dogs. If you want one of these dogs for a pet with some genuine character, any will suffice. If you want one of these dogs for use as a pet and home guardian, any dog over 55 pounds will work well. If you want one of these dogs so that you'll have the toughest dog in the neighborhood, you're probably too late. These days everybody has a backyard-bred Pit Bull and many of these are tough. If you feel that you don't want a dog that won't be the toughest dog in the neighborhood, let me suggest to you that perhaps it isn't a dog that you want at all, but rather something else. I suggest that you make a pilgrimage to a mountain top somewhere and try to find peace.

Finally, the academic answer: The truth is that the primary reason it doesn't make sense to rank the fighting breeds, as opposed to ranking dogs from within one breed, is that you will inevitably be comparing apples to oranges. The American Pit Bull Terrier, at its best, is an extremely powerful, capable dog. The Tosa Token, at its best, is an extremely powerful, capable dog. To watch Japanese Tosa matches is an awe-inspiring experience. To watch a Pit Bull match is also incredibly awe-inspiring. For that matter, to watch a top-quality working American Bulldog hit a wild hog is so awe-inspiring that it never ceases to send a chill up my spine, and I have told others on many occasions that if you watch a video of such an event and it doesn't literally send a chill up your spine as well, you undoubtedly have no real appreciation of working dogs.

Tosa Token wearing a Yokozuna championship collar, owned by Mr. Yokoshima of Japan.

But when each of these breeds is doing what it has been bred to do, it is doing something very different than that which any other breed does. The American Bulldog is a working dog. Some of the gamest American Bulldogs on the face of the earth are primarily hog dogs. Hog doggers are not interested in owning a Bulldog that is interested in attacking other dogs for the simple reason that when the Bulldog is released to catch a hog that is surrounded by a pack of hounds that has brought that hog to bay, its the hog and not one of the hounds that the Bulldog is expected to be focused upon.

The Tosa dog has been selectively bred for over a century to fight according to the rules of the Japanese dog match. The rules of the Japanese dog match are not the same as the rules of the underground Pit Bull match as it is conducted in this country and elsewhere. Each dog is great at what it does. In order to do well according to Japanese rules, dogs are often bred to be very large. In the United States, and where Pit Bull matches are staged elsewhere, smaller dogs are admired and often more highly regarded. As such, why is it necessary to simply throw them all into a cage together and see which dog ultimately comes out alive? What will this teach us that we don't already know? Why would we prize a 160-pound Tosa or a 200-pound Tosa more highly than we would the 55-pound Pit Bull it killed, but barely?

For the benefit of those who have cornered me on this question and who don't care about apples and oranges but only about which dog will win in the end, I must tell you that in addition to there being some very accomplished fighting Pit Bulls out there, there are also some very capable "dog game bred" American Bulldogs as well. Additionally, there are some really devastating Tosas. The Tosa's game is a very short one. The Pit Bull's game is generally a very long one. The American Bulldog's game is in between. Of the three, I have always most admired the Pit Bull, but I have heard stories from reliable sources that many an American Bulldog has earned the respect of many a serious dog fighter. Who knows? Maybe, in the end, the single toughest dog alive is some especially ornery Great Dane sitting in someone's backyard somewhere.

The author with "The Puppy from Mars," a little
Shar-Pei pup belonging to Eddie Dombish of New
York City. Get a look at the face on this thing! It looks
unreal, doesn't it?! (The dog's face, that is.)

Q: Do you fight dogs yourself?
A: No I don't. I have never had any desire to enter a dog
in a fight and it is highly doubtful that I ever will. Having
said this, let me assure you that there are many people who
will never believe what I just said and I have a funny story
about just such a person. One day when my mother was still
alive and well, she read about a rare-breed show that was
to be held in a bank in midtown Manhattan. On a whim,
having nothing to do that afternoon, she decided to get on
the subway and go to the show. When she got there, she saw
that one of the breeds on exhibition was the Chinese Shar-
Pei and that there was a man associated with the breed at
the show dispensing "expert" information about Shar-Peis.

My mother walked over to the man, watched the dog he was displaying for a while, and then casually said, "Oh, yes, I read all about this breed in a book called *The World Of Fighting Dogs*," at which point the guy with the Shar-Pei proceeded to tell my mother that he knows people who know of the guy who wrote that book and that he's a dog fighter like none other. When my mother pointed out that "the author" had stated quite clearly in the book that he was not a dog fighter, the Shar-Pei's owner replied, "Well, what else would you expect him to say? There are laws against dogfighting you know." My mother got quite a kick out of that stupid conversation and never did tell the guy that I was her son.

What would I say to a guy like that, assuming that I had any desire to say anything at all to a guy like that? This is America where we Americans can say whatever we like, for the time being. If I did fight dogs, I'd say so. If I was afraid of drawing attention to myself, I certainly would not be writing books like this one, appearing on radio and television to talk about fighting dogs, etc. Let's face it, I could not have drawn more attention to the fact that I am interested in these fighting dogs if a flew a huge, hot air balloon over my house declaring the fact in bold print. The fact is that I don't fight dogs. If you are more comfortable viewing me as being someone who enjoys blood sports, let me give you some valid ammunition, I am a passionate deer hunter. There is nothing I enjoy more than hunting deer with a heavy caliber, muzzle-loading rifle. Take me to task about that, if you feel an urge to take me to task, but in accusing me of fighting dogs, you'll be "barking up the wrong tree," so to speak.

Q : If you don't fight dogs, how can I be sure that your breeding program is producing game dogs?

A: I don't have a breeding program. I don't breed dogs. I have gotten owners of dogs who wanted to breed together, but I have never bred a dog of my own, with the exception of one breeding of my old Bullmastiff.

Tom Garner's Chinaman Buddy, owned by Paul Kunkel of Helsinki, Finland. Paul calls the dog Napsu. Tom Garner has emerged as another serious player in the world of quality Pit Bull breeding.

Q: Why haven't you bred any dogs of your own?

A: No time. No room. Don't enjoy cleaning dog poop. Don't want the headaches associated with selling puppies. Also, I have always much preferred to have only one dog in the house. I like the relationship that forms between a family and its one and only dog better than I do the relationship which forms between any one dog of a number of dogs and the family that owns those dogs. We have had two dogs in the past and we will undoubtedly have two again, but this is purely due to the fact that while my wife and I both enjoy owning a dog, compromise about the kind of dog we should own has proven to be absolutely impossible.

Q. If you don't fight dogs yourself, how can you condone the fact that others fight dogs?

A: I believe there are no greater hypocrites on the face of the earth than those people who are forever going on and on about how barbaric dogfighting is and how cruel it is, and how strongly they oppose it, and then they go out and buy themselves a Pit Bull pup (or a pup from any other of the fighting breeds). Where in the world do these people think their dog came from? It is a product of the dog pits, and if they like the dog, then they like the effect that the dog pits have had upon their dog's character. Personally, I have never condoned dogfighting—I have simply admitted that whatever it was that gave rise to some of the great gladiator breeds, it worked well to produce a great companion as well. I would think that anyone who truly opposed the sport of dogfighting would see to it that he did not support it by selecting as his own family dog the product of the dog fighter's game.

Cody, the author's old Bullmastiff, was a sweet family
pet that didn't live to be four years of age. Cancer
was the cause of his death.

Q. What kind of dog do you own?

A. I've had a number of dogs. I had my white Pit Bull, Nugget, for just short of 14 years. I took a break of a few months after Nugget died and I bought an eight-week-old Bullmastiff puppy. We named him Cody. He grew to be 130 pounds or so and died at age four of some horrendous immune system deficiency. He was a nice, teddy bear of a pet but I wouldn't get another Bullmastiff as the problems we had with poor Cody's health completely put me off the breed. In truth, he was a knucklehead anyway, so no matter how healthy he was, I would have been put off the breed at the end.

After Cody I again took a break of a few months and then I brought home a very young American Staffordshire Terrier pup. If I remember right, Spike had just turned four weeks old the day I brought him home. As far as I am concerned, this is much too young to take a pup away from its mother and siblings and I took him in spite of my better judgment because the woman who owned him simply gets rid of pups as soon as they take their first bite of food. To make matters worse, this particular pup had no tail because it had been stomped off when its mother had gotten into a fight with another adult dog right in the whelping box. Most of the pups had been killed, but Spike survived, tailless. To make a long story short, the dog had had such poor early socialization that he never did grow up right. I never liked his attitude and when he turned ten months old, I gave him back to the woman who had given him to me. I had no regrets about getting rid of Spike. He was no dog for a family.

After Spike we had a number of dogs come and go but only one was brought here with the idea of keeping it. There was an Australian Cattle Dog that loved me and hated

The author's son Dan with Gumbo, the family's Catahoula Bulldog. Here Gumbo was six months of age.

anything else that moved. He lives on a ranch out west now. This is a perfect environment for a dog like him. There was a French Bulldog that a friend owned. The Frenchie lived in a kennel at a dog grooming shop and I felt sorry for him so I brought him home just to see to it that he would enjoy a bit of its life anyway. The kids liked him but he wasn't ours to keep. There was a Bull Terrier that had come in from Moscow in the former Soviet Union. Crash was in the process of being "dumped," more or less because his owner just couldn't handle him. She wanted to sell him cheap so I bought him with an eye toward selling him for no profit just to see to it he would get a good home. This worked out well for Crash as I did find him a good home, but he ended up spending more time with us than I had originally anticipated. It was okay.

Finally there was Gumbo, the big Catahoula Bulldog I raised from puppyhood. Gumbo was an interesting and ultimately sad story. His father was a huge, powerful American Bulldog. His mother was supposedly pure

Catahoula Leopard Dog. I saw the mother and to me she looked like she had some Bulldog in her too, but who knows. Gumbo was a gift from a good friend of mine, namely Chief Gerry Pleasant of the Hartford, Connecticut, police force.

I got Gumbo when he was eight weeks old or so. He had been very well socialized as a young pup and he came home with us as a classic tail-wagging, kid-loving pup. As he grew he became a great home guardian, the kind of dog that would wag his tail furiously whenever he saw any young child on the street (I love a dog like that), the kind of dog that would always position himself between me and anyone I stopped to chat with on the street or anyone who came to our home, simply because he wanted to be sure that I was protected from unforeseen attack, and the kind of dog who always had to be in contact with me. (If I got up to go to the bathroom, Gumbo had to come with me. If I sat down on the couch in the den, Gumbo had to fall asleep with his head on my feet.) And he was the kind of dog who loved to hike in the woods, a favorite pastime of mine as well.

In spite of the fact that Gumbo was coming up so well, I knew that deep down inside he was a tough dog. I made sure that he always knew who was boss. This is why when Gumbo was turning ten months old or so and we were going away on a vacation on which he couldn't join us, I made plans to leave Gumbo with a professional attack trainer friend of mine. I knew Eddie would know how to handle Gumbo and that Gumbo would respect Eddie as his boss until I returned.

On the day that we were leaving for vacation and I was preparing to bring Gumbo to Eddie's place, my next-door neighbor, who would be watching my wife's little dog, approached me and asked me why I was willing to separate the two dogs. He pleaded to watch both dogs and promised that he'd obey any rules I laid down concerning how Gumbo was to be treated. He assured me that he would use a firm hand and not allow Gumbo to rule the roost. I guess the temptation to keep the two dogs together, right next door, and not to have Gumbo kenneled the entire time we were gone was strong. Against my better judgment, I gave in and left both dogs with my neighbor.

I knew I was in trouble the minute I got home two weeks later. I ran right next door to reclaim Gumbo and my neighbor immediately assured me that Gumbo was fine and had had a great time in my absence. He did admit, a little sheepishly, that he had let the rules slip a bit, however. I knew this meant trouble. I asked what rules had slipped and what the dog's reaction had been. The neighbor advised me that Gumbo had been fed at the table, had been allowed to sleep on the furniture, and even to sleep in bed. He went so far as to tell me that one night he had found Gumbo sleeping in his bed and when he tried to evict the dog from the bed, the dog had growled at him. When I asked what he had done in response to the growl he said simply, "I slept in the other room." I knew for sure then that we were in deep trouble.

I brought Gumbo home more or less completely out of control. He had long since decided that he had made a mistake while living with me and that in fact, it was the family dog who was the boss of the house. I knew I could correct the situation and I also knew that it would take time and a great deal of work. I knew that in the meantime, Gumbo was one dangerous dog to have in the house with young kids and strange adults coming and going regularly.

For no better reason than that, I couldn't find a good

home for Gumbo immediately, I kenneled him, I worked with him and, with some hard correction, I fixed the problem almost completely. I got him to a point at which I no longer felt he would kill the mailman if I slipped but once, that he would not kill guests to the house, and that the in-laws could come to the house in my absence without fearing for their lives. However, the first time I brought Gumbo to a piece of woods that both he and I knew well, his failure to follow basic commands immediately upon hearing them brought about his swift demise.

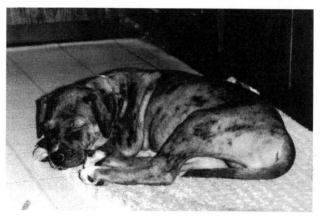

Gumbo asleep. As an adult, this dog was an awe-some guard dog.

My son Alex, Gumbo, and I had been hiking for hours. Before heading back to the car we decided to top one more hill, the hill Alex and I call "Buck Hill" because we are always assured of spotting an eight-point buck up there along with a doe or two and often some fine wild turkeys. We saw our buck and eight turkeys and sat down on a log for a rest before hiking back to the car. It had always been my habit to allow

Gumbo considerable liberty because, by and large, he was a very obedient dog. That day, Gumbo was not as tired as Alex and I were, so he decided to take a walk, mark a tree here and there, and pick up a few scents.

The last time I ever saw Gumbo he was dropping out of site over a ridge. I knew when he walked down the other side of the ridge we'd lose sight of him so I whistled my "Get Over Here!" whistle to him. He never even looked at me. I called his name, in no uncertain terms. Again he didn't look at me. Finally, Alex and I got up and took off after Gumbo. We never saw him again. Days later we got a call from the local police. They informed us that Gumbo had been hit by a car and killed instantly, two miles from where we had last seen him and within a couple of hundred yards of where we had parked our car.

That was the end of Gumbo. Willy, my wife's dog, missed him for weeks. My sons both missed him too. Barbara was shocked when she saw us pull up in front of the house without him, holding his empty leash in my hand. But, I guess that's the way it goes. Am I sorry I allowed him to run off lead? No. A life at the end of a chain all the time is no life for a dog. I've had many dogs who have been very happy roaming in the woods off lead. Instead, what I'm sorry about, is that I hadn't left Gumbo with someone who had more experience dealing with tough, dominant dogs. That was my fatal error. Anyway, before long it'll be time for a new dog. Right now I'm looking at Korean Jindo Dogs, Pit Bulls, and American Bulldogs (if I can find one small and hard enough among all of today's froggy slobs). Either dog will suffice, as will almost any breed discussed in this book.

East End Boy, a Dublin Red Staffy Bull,
sired by a good dog from Sweden.

Q. Why did you say in your second book that of all breeds you like the Pit Bull best?

A. The Pit Bull, or the American Pit Bull Terrier, is the most of what I like in the smallest possible package. Among guard-dog and gladiator-breed enthusiasts, only the novices prefer the largest dog they can find, unless the breed in question is one of the Mastiffs and intended to be large. When I had my Bullmastiff, as sweet a dog as he was, I felt like I'd gone into the business of raising livestock.

Eve of Joyce, a Staffy Bull from Sweden, a double-bred Josh bitch, owned by Magnus Paulsson.

I had a 130-pound dog in my house at all times, when a 60-pound dog would have been every bit as capable of deterring an intruder. There was no reason for the beastly size. It only made the dog difficult to walk and disgusting to have in the car.

The Pit Bull, as opposed to the American Staffordshire Terrier, is occasionally still bred to be a performance dog. Unlike many dogs that are bred for no other reason than to look good, and so to win shows, the game-bred Pit Bull must have a brain. I much prefer a dog with a brain. Dogs without brains, like my poor Bullmastiff, are for people who expect virtually nothing from their pet. I prefer a pet that can offer me intelligent companionship, and so a brain is required.

In recent years, due to a tremendous growth in popularity of dog shows featuring Pit Bulls, I have witnessed a surge in the number of brainless Pit Bulls. This phenomenon, as unfortunate as it might be, does not surprise me. The American dog-show scene does not select for brains, as dog shows throughout much of Europe do, and so this illusive quality (intelligence) appears with less and less frequency and on lower and lower levels. Ultimately we end up with dogs, of whatever breed, that are purely "showbrained," to use an expression that I made up years ago and that I will coin now.

But many an intelligent Pit Bull still exists, and this intelligence, combined with the loyalty that is typical of a Pit Bull, the strength that is unequaled in the world of dogs, the courage that defines the breed, and the determination that has become proverbial, is what I like about Pit Bulls.

Pit Bull speaking out at a dog show.

Q. What size dog is necessary for man-stopping purposes?
A. That depends upon the dog. A Boston Terrier may scare a man but when that man gets mad because he fears for his safety, you had better have a powerful dog if you intend to stop him. A man experiencing that kind of adrenaline blast can be a powerful adversary. A 60-pound Pit Bull may be able to stop a man, but a 60-pound dog of a lesser breed may well

find itself in terrible trouble when it first hurts a scared and angry man. If you feel you may need a dog to actually stop a man, you are better off with too much dog than with too little. It's no wonder that when the gamekeepers of England decided they needed a dog that could stop a man who was being pursued under penalty of death, they felt it necessary to develop the Bullmastiff of old. After all, what else could stop such a man who was fighting for his life?

Gizella Dirigent, a five-year-old Bull Terrier bitch from Russia owned by Bunina Tanya. The author thinks this is one good-looking bitch.

Q. How can you say that the Bull Terrier is not a game dog? Why I knew a Bull Terrier once... (This question came to me most recently from a reader in Ferntree Gully, Australia. Sounds like it would be a nice place, doesn't it? Apparently the Bull Terrier is still used for catch work there.)

A. The term "gameness," as it is used by dog fighters, means something very specific. It means that a dog has been born, as a result of highly selective breeding for the quality of gameness, with an atavistic tendency to fight in spite of the odds being overwhelmingly stacked against it. This quality of gameness is a very illusive one. Just as dogs of the larger breeds tend to diminish in size unless attention is paid in the breeding program, and just as short-faced dogs tend to become longer-faced dogs unless a breeding program is pursued to select forthe shorter-faced dogs, dogs that are not game in any given line of game dogs tend to arise more and more frequently unless a breeder is game testing his line and then selecting for game dogs in his breeding program.

There are qualities in a dog that nature does not like. The quality of continuing to attack an adversary even though a dog is being hurt in this pursuit is one of these qualities. It doesn't make sense from the point of view of staying alive and giving oneself the opportunity to procreate. But in a breeding program aimed at establishing and perpetuating game dogs, man has taken the role of nature and introduced a new demand into the dog's environment. This demand is that if a dog is going to procreate, *i.e.*, give rise to puppies that will mature to be like itself, it must fight, no matter what. This is the quality that is being selected for and so this is the quality that is being perpetuated and so again, this is the quality typical of a good Pit Bull.

Once, a long time ago, the Bull Terrier, as a breed, was game tested and bred according to its ability in the dog pits rather than being bred for its looks. With rare exception, this has not been the case for a long time and so this quality of gameness is not nearly as prevalent among dogs of this breed

31

as it once was. Does this mean that there can never be any such thing as a game Bull Terrier again? Not at all. A "throw back" can occur. This is to say that as this is a quality that was once typical of the breed, it would be a mistake to think that it is now definitely completely gone from the Bull Terrier gene pool. A game dog could crop up here and there, though not as frequently as game-bred Pit Bulls, however.

Let me end this answer by saying that true gameness is rare, even among game-bred dogs. As the instinct to survive is strong, the tendency to simply throw in the towel when a dog is getting tired and hurt is strong too. Even among dogs that are potentially game in a pit-fighting situation, many fine pets have cropped up. While a highly game-bred dog might not be as wise a choice for a family pet that a Golden Retriever generally is, a game-bred, inexperienced fighting dog can often endear itself to its owner or owners in the right situation. To view any dog that was game bred as being always dangerous to man is foolish.

Q. Why didn't you include some of the better known "fighting breeds," such as the Boston Terrier, the English and the French Bulldog, the Boxer, etc., in your first book?

A. Frankly, this question was not asked of me as frequently as I had thought it would be. I think readers intuitively understood that the first book was a book about those fighting breeds that the average purebred dog enthusiast knew too little about. As such, it was a book about those fighting breeds that remained functionally capable enough (highly spirited enough, if you will) to at very least remind the observer that they had once been (and in some instances still were) capable gladiators.

When one looks at the average, show-variety English Bulldog, the gladiator history of this breed does not immediately leap to mind. Similarly, the French Bulldog, the Boxer, and others, as these breeds appear to us today, are not what one would expect of a functionally capable breed. These breeds do exist today and the dogs representing them are, in fact, the direct descendants of the great gladiator breeds of old, but if it's purely history you are interested in, you can find that written elsewhere. I didn't want my book to be a rehashing of that information.

I wanted to present new information about little-known breeds. I wanted to write a book that would offer information that had not been offered before. Hopefully, this book will have that in common with my first book. Incidentally, you may have noticed that I did not include a chapter on the Shar-Pei breed in this book either, although I did discuss these dogs in my first book. The Shar-Pei has been embraced exclusively by the show world, and while I don't dislike these dogs, they don't especially interest me either. Each to his own. Some Boxers, French Bulldogs, and Boston Terriers do interest me still.

Q. What breeds are being actively fought in dog pits throughout the United States today?

A. This is an interesting question because what the novice in this area may think of as being "a dogfight" is not necessarily what an experienced dog fighter views as being a dogfight. To illustrate how confusing this can be for some people, let me tell you that a woman I once knew, who was editor-in-chief of a major American dog magazine, once got really upset with me when I told her that such breeds as Doberman Pinschers, German Shepherds, etc., are not used as fighting

Here's NYC's own, former Mayor Ed Koch, who was gracious
enough to send this photograph with a brindle Boxer that he
brought back from Germany after his service in WWII. New York-
ers think of the charasmatic Koch as having served as Mayor for
a longer period of time than any other, but few are aware that he
saw heavy action during the war. Koch speaks of it humbly. This
tough old-style German Boxer is an appropriate dog for this
courageous man.

dogs. She swore up and down that she had personally rescued some Dobermans from the dog pits and declared that, had it not been for her, these animals would have spent their lives as fighting dogs in the hands of merciless dog fighters who would have traveled the country betting all kinds of money on their Doberman's ability to kill other dogs.

I told this woman that while she may have found someone, somewhere who fought dogs once and who was inexperienced enough in the area of organized dogfighting that he didn't know that Dobermans weren't fighting dogs, and that she may, in fact, have done these dogs a favor by rescuing them from this idiot, finding Dobermans in the dog pits was certainly the exception rather than the rule. Dobermans were bred for reasons other than for dogfighting. They are fine at doing what they were bred to do, but they would not last as fighting dogs. The Doberman, as a breed, is not, has never been, and undoubtedly will never be the pit fighter's dog of choice.

She was furious, and years later I believe she still is. She had really wanted to believe that she had put a dent in organized dogfighting by doing whatever it was she had done. She wanted very much to believe that her breed of choice, the Doberman Pinscher, was a fighting breed and that she was a major champion of the breed, fighting to save the breed from unscrupulous dog fighters. Many Bullmastiff owners and breeders feel the same way. Rottweiler owners and breeders often do too. I suppose when selling puppies it's better to be too cautious rather than not cautious enough, but it has been my impression that owners and breeders of non-fighting breeds sometimes prefer to view their dogs as fighting breeds that are widely discriminated against. They seem to enjoy wringing their hands, pounding their chests and wailing "Why would anyone want to hurt my Fido?" You would think that if they wanted to play this role, they would simply get themselves a Pit Bull. Who can explain what's going on in the mind of another?

Anyway, in answer to the original question, the vast majority of today's organized dog fighters are fighting Pit Bulls. In recent years, American Bulldogs have found their way to the dog pits in greater numbers than ever before. Also, the Tosa dog of Japan, actively fought in the dogfighting arenas of Japan since they were developed, is now, on occasion, being fought in the United States. The results of American Bulldog matches are actually occasionally published these days as well. The bottom line here is that there are some really tough American Bulldogs out there, but that these matches do not go on for the great length of time that Pit Bull matches do, for the most part.

Before ending this, I would like to mention that I have been hearing scattered reports about Americans using Argentine Dogos in matches against Pit Bulls and American Bulldogs. While these matches are very infrequent, they occur often enough and, where they do occur they are conducted by people experienced enough, that this deserves mention. In every such situation that has been described to me, the results have been the same. The Dogo lost. Every time I have had this told to me I have responded in the same way. I've asked, "What in the world are you fighting Dogos for? These are not fighting dogs. They are great at what they do, when they're good, and this is good enough." I guess these dogs look so much like huge white Pit Bulls that even experienced dog fighters have gotten curious as to how they would do in a match. Well, the jury is back, the verdict is in, and everybody can stop fighting Dogos now!

Q. Why don't you feel that a Pit Bull/Rottweiler cross is an important one? (This question has cropped up now and then over the years, but it came to me most recently from Joe Northington of Brooklyn, New York.)

A. I don't see where you are benefiting either the Pit Bull breed or the Rottweiler breed by crossing these two dogs. Rotties are fine as they are, if you like that kind of dog. Pit Bulls are fine as they are too. What is the advantage of having a cross between the two? There was a time when Pit Bulls were much smaller. My Nugget was a 66-pound dog, soaking wet, and when I had him he was considered very large. Now we live in the day of the 100-pound, "pure-bred" Pit Bull, so why cross a Pit Bull to a Rottweiler?

The following letter came to me from a legal firm in Alabama. I will let you read some of it here, witness the question put to me, and then answer the question here as I did on the telephone with the attorney who asked for my help. By the way, he seemed like a nice enough fellow, and I really got the sense that he was writing to ask a question rather than to extract from me the answer he wanted.

Dear Mr. Semencic,

I am an attorney representing (name omitted) who are the parents of a young boy who was attacked and disfigured by an Akita last year. My investigation into this matter has revealed that the dog was allowed to roam at large on the premises of its owner while children were at play, even though it had been trained as a guard dog and behaved aggressively toward people and animals in the past.

In preparing this case for trial in June, I have reviewed some articles on dog attacks, have consulted with several animal behaviorists, and have learned that Akitas are inherently aggressive dogs....

Also, I am interested in learning your opinions on the nature of Akitas and whether they have any genetically determined characteristics that make them inclined to behave viciously or aggressively.

A. As you may have noticed, I have chosen to ignore questions that pertain to any particular breed in this question-and-answer section. I have paraphrased this question here because although the questioner viewed it as a question specific to the Akita breed, I view it as a question that could have been, and in fact has been asked of me, pertaining to every breed discussed in my first book.

I think it is extremely sad when a person, particularly a child, is hurt or killed by a dog. I think that honest accidents occasionally happen, the result of which are that a child is hurt by a dog. For example, I have heard of situations in which a person who lived in a bad area genuinely feared for his life, and for good reason, because a rash of break-ins in that area resulted in homeowners being hurt or killed by criminals. In response to the need for protection at home, some owners have opted to get a large, scary, aggressive, "serious" dog, sometimes from among the fighting breeds and sometimes not. In fact, when burglars have been interviewed and asked what is the single greatest deterrent against break-in, the overwhelming majority have stated that large-aggressive dogs are very likely to cause a burglar to look elsewhere for his next meal.

Yet I have known of situations in which a dog was obtained for protection and the "intruder" the dog sank its teeth into was not a burglar but a neighbor's child chasing a ball. This, I would say, is not a "crime" on anyone's part but rather a horrible accident. Horrible accidents do occasionally happen, and while we could argue that with the proper precautionary measures effected, even these could be largely avoided, the list of otherwise useful items we would have to eliminate from our lives in order to do so would leave us living in an unhappy, overly governed world.

The situation described above doesn't sound like an honest accident to me, given what little I know of the story, however. But it is not reasonable to blame this disaster on society's allowing an "inherently aggressive" breed of dog, the Akita, or whatever breed, to live among us. If we wanted to point a finger at a breed as being "inherently aggressive," we could make a case that most of today's purebreds have histories, which render them "inherently aggressive." When we begin to point this finger, where and how do we stop pointing it? All coursing hounds were selectively bred to pursue a hunter's prey. Certainly they would all be the first to go, wouldn't they? The Doberman, the Bullmastiff and others were bred specifically to attack man. Possibly they should be the first to be disallowed. Of all pure bred-dogs in New York City and possibly throughout the country, do you know which has proven itself most likely to bite people, on a per capita basis? Not the Akita or the Pit Bull, but rather the Cocker Spaniel! I have heard the argument that the Cocker can't inflict serious damage upon a person when it does attack, but certainly none of the parents of young children who have been seriously mauled would agree. Should Cockers then be the first to go in our campaign to eliminate all inherently dangerous dogs from our society?

We as a society can't run from everything. We can try to make ourselves look good in the eyes of others by proposing that "potentially dangerous aspects of our society" be eliminated, but this is an extremely naive view of problem solving. Besides, we decided years ago that recreational drugs were dangerous and so should be made totally illegal, and

A particularly fine Dogo Argentino, handled by Drew M. Marszal of Dogo de Suenos kennels in Florida.

where has that gotten us? Passing laws against them have only forced us to realize that we are unable to enforce such laws.

I told the attorney that I thought he was making a mistake in focusing his efforts on proving that the Akita is an inherently dangerous breed and that owning one is an irresponsible act. I told him that from the little he had described to me of the situation, two questions leaped out at me. First, why was this dog maintained in such an irresponsible manner? If the dog was aggressive, why was he allowed to roam among children unattended? Second, who had attack-trained this Akita and then put it in the hands of an owner who apparently didn't realize how dangerous an attack-trained dog, especially a poorly attack-trained dog, could be?

If we as a society are going to maintain any liberties at all, we must learn to be responsible adults. Those among us who feel they have a need or a desire to own a dog like the ones discussed in this book must accept the fact that these, and other dogs, must be owned responsibly. Responsibility is the first thing one must assume when one decides to own a powerful or even a not so powerful animal.

You are reading my book.

Perhaps you have read dog books by me before. As such, I think it's safe to assume that you think there is at least a good possibility that I know what I am talking about with regard to dogs. If so, keep firmly in mind that though I may keep large and powerful dogs in my home and living among my children, I am extremely watchful at all times of the dog's attitude toward others.

I allow my dogs no liberties that could lead to a dangerous

situation for anyone. I am known by the "dog people" who know me as being extremely careful, and sometimes maybe too careful, with my dogs. I will not hesitate to immediately get rid of a dog that appears that it could be a danger to anyone but an intruder or an attacker, or become a liability to me. I think any ownership of any powerful animal requires that you employ a similar strategy and if you do not, and if anyone is hurt as a result of your negligence, then both barrels of the law should be aimed at you long before they are aimed at any breed of dog.

Q. *What is your doctorate in? Are you a veterinarian?*

A. No, I'm not a vet. I think, if I were a vet, I'd call myself Carl Semencic, DVM, wouldn't I? Isn't that what vets do? My doctorate is in anthropology. My area of specialization was early man in the new world. This question comes to me very regularly, most recently today.

Q. *If you are so interested in these "fighting dogs," why don't you fight dogs yourself?*

A. I don't know what kind of person I'd be if I had a great deal of time on my hands and enough real estate to keep a kennel. Living in New York City, I've spent most of my life in apartments and, in recent years, in a house that sits on a 60' by 100' piece of property. Furthermore, I've always been a busy guy.

Being in this position, I have never had any inclination or ability to own more than one good dog at a time. As such, the relationship that develops between me and the dog is not one in which either of us has any desire to see the other fighting for his life in a pit. My dogs and I become buddies, and that's it.

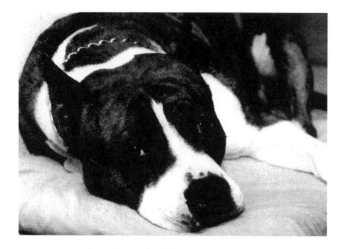

American Staffordshire Terrier,
Tough Guy's April, owned and bred by Guenther
Haas of Austria.

By the way, the fact that I have never had a great deal of property undoubtedly also explains my preference for smaller dogs.

Q. How did you learn so much about dogs?

A. Believe me, if you had spent the last 25 years intensely interested in dogs and talking to purebred-dog enthusiasts verbally, via computer online services, letters, etc., you would have learned a few things about dogs too. Also, I've forgotten who it was who originally said this but I am quoting someone else who said this really insightful thing once. He said, "If you ever want to learn all there is to know about a subject, write a book about it." This is true. I had a very hard time collecting the information that went into that first book, but once the book had been published, information began to pour in from all over the world and it has never stopped coming. You wouldn't believe how many people in how many places

I have corresponded with over the years. You just wouldn't believe it.

I'll tell you something else. This dog subject isn't exactly rocket science. There are many purebred enthusiasts out there for whom their knowledge of this subject is a great claim to fame, but the fact is that this is just lots of common "dog talk." In an effort to entertain my elder son's budding interests, I have taken out family memberships in both the New York Paleontological Society and the New York Herpetological Society. I have been amazed at how much some of these bright amateurs have learned about their respective areas of interest. Some hobbyists really become involved in what they're doing.

Q. Why are you so interested in fighting dogs?

A. It never ceases to amaze me that this question would even occur to anyone and yet it comes to me all the time, most recently via an e-mail from a lady named Psyche Williams, who is apparently a Rhodesian Ridgeback breeder. The reason the question puzzles me and strikes me as being an invalid one is that it is not asked of those who own dogs in other categories or "groups." After all, the number of dogs of all groups used in a "working" environment (i.e., used for the working purpose for which the breed in question was originally developed) is extremely small compared to the number of those dogs simply kept as pets. Yet when was the last time you heard the kind of suspicion expressed toward those who keep so many of these other dogs that is expressed toward owners of "the fighting dogs."

For example, when is the last time you heard of someone walking up to the owner of a Bloodhound and asking,

The Dogue de Bordeaux is less rare these days
than when the author first published his chapter on
them in *The World of Fighting Dogs*. Three fine Park
Avenue Bordeaux: Ubu, Patrick and Oscar.

with suspicion plastered all over his or her face as well as
in his or her voice, "Why would you feel a need to own a
Bloodhound? Do you track fugitives for a living?" Or when
is the last time you witnessed someone asking the owner of a
German Shepherd or a Collie why he or she would want to
own a dog that brings people sheep?

If this question sounds foolish when asked of owners of
dogs like these and so many others, why doesn't it sound
equally foolish when it is asked of a Pit Bull owner? It's
understood that most German Shepherd dogs are not
owned by German sheep herders, but rather they are owned
by people who simply enjoy keeping these dogs as pets. It
is understood that most Irish Wolfhounds are not kept by
active hunters of Irish wolves, but rather that the primary

purpose of these dogs is to lay on the rug and be friendly. So why is it so rarely understood that the average "fighting dog" is kept by a person or a family who simply feels like keeping it because they like it?

To make matters even more complicated, it seems that the breed type of the fighting dog owned makes a difference in the collective mind of those who feel a need to criticize fighting-dog ownership. For example, I have yet to hear anyone ask an owner of the AKC show-variety English Bulldog why he or she would want to own a fighting (or bull-baiting) dog. I suppose this is primarily due to the fact that, actual breed history notwithstanding, it is widely recognized and understood that the English Bulldog is no longer physically or temperamentally equipped to latch on to a raging bull and hang until the bull collapses. It is widely understood that these dogs are bred to be grotesque, and that's all, and that they are owned by people who like this grotesque appearance.

In consideration of this fact, one might speculate that it is the actual ability of some of today's fighting breeds that puts suspicion in the mind of some. Then we would have to go on to ask if this is so, why it is not also so that the average person is suspicious of the owners of Border Collies, Australian Cattle Dogs, Chesapeake Bay Retrievers, etc., many of which remain functionally capable animals. Yet no one seems to be the least bit curious about owners and enthusiasts of these breeds. Suspicion remains directed at owners of the fighting breeds alone.

I will never fully understand why the average person does not more readily recognize the lack of reason behind asking this question about only one group of dogs. To me, the question is meaningless and so the answer is a very simple one. It is "Why wouldn't I want to own a fighting dog?" or perhaps "What is it about you that makes you suspicious of only the fighting breeds?" They're a strange bunch, these hunters of witches. They're a strange bunch, to be sure.

Q. Why did you say, in your second book, Pit Bulls and Tenacious Guard Dogs, *that you felt that in the long run it would be in European countries where such breeds as the American Bulldog, and others, would survive in their purest form?*

A. This is a really complicated question because its answer is manyfold. Let me take a crack at answering it.

First, at the time I wrote my second book, I was very disenchanted with the direction taken by many breeders of many of the dogs I had discussed in my first book, the American Bulldog in particular. One breeder was working furiously at producing a great hog-catching dog, while another was working just as furiously at producing a great fighting dog, and yet another was working to produce the largest, fattest slob of a dog that he possibly could. I thought that perhaps, if some more rigid "let's do it by the book" type German or Dutchman, would take the best of the stock (American Bulldog, Pit Bull, etc.) we had available at the time, isolate it, and simply work hard with it, that country would learn to appreciate "the dog" in its purest, most traditional, most meaningful form.

To some extent, I was correct in this idea. From what I have observed, and from what my many European contacts tell me, in Europe there is less diversity of type within each breed exported from the United States. European, and to some extent Asian, breeders have proven themselves to be more concerned with the preservation of the original type and have been more likely to resent trendy typological swings. American breeders of American Bulldogs have not been as diligent in this area In fact, they may simply be too close to the source of information. They hear the rumors about who is breeding what other breed into his American Bulldog lines and this justifies their own desire to add a little something to their own American Bulldog lines as well. To the best of my knowledge, being farther away from the rumor mill has helped maintain greater purity among American Bulldog lines that have found their ways to other countries.

Secondly, European breeders and show judges are more concerned with maintaining the functional qualities of a breed than we Americans are. I have no desire to come down as hard on the AKC as I have in the past because as the fighting breeds have come under attack, it had been the legal arm of the AKC which has proven itself to be the best friend imaginable of the owners of the fighting breeds. They have opposed breed-specific legislation on all fronts and as such, they have proven to be our friends.

However, I will point out that the AKC, and other major, American, purebred registry organizations, do not test for a breed's functional ability when determining championship. They merely establish and document a dog's compliance with a written standard for the excellence of its appearance. I would argue that form should follow function in each case in which a breed standard is established and that without some test for function, we can never know if our current form is meaningful. In any event, the AKC does not register the American Bulldog, but this attitude that form alone is enough to determine the quality of a dog, pervades all of American dogdom, and American dogdom is largely presided over by the AKC.

Many European registry organizations test for functional ability before awarding a championship. This is another reason that lead me to think that Europeans would be better at preserving true breed type than we would. Yet, in retrospect, it's obvious to me that while they might test for function, they will not be testing for the function of our breeds. They will not match Pit Bulls before determining championship. They will not be putting an American Bull on a hog before determining championship. They will simply test a dog for its willingness and for its physical ability to attack a man. I don't think this is enough.

The Pit Bull is often a great man-stopper, but "man-stopping" is not what those breeders who created and who preserved this breed cared about. The Pit Bull is a dog that was bred and preserved for one reason and one reason only—to defeat all canine opponents in the dog pits. European judges are not testing for this ability and neither will they be doing so in the near future. As such, what is the value of what they are doing?

Thirdly, I made a big mistake! I panicked. I witnessed the irrational decision making that was giving rise to anti-Pit Bull (and related breed) legislation throughout the United States, and I decided that clearer heads might prevail elsewhere in the world. I don't know how I could have conceived this idea. It's here in the United States where liberty still means something. Granted, it doesn't mean what it once did, and granted, the situation looks pretty bleak on many fronts, but we are still "the land of the free" after all. I can't imagine that I could have forgotten this, but I did.

Throughout much of the world, breed-specific legislation was put into effect even as rumors that a breed might be coming to a country were spread. In England, for example, Pit Bulls were totally banned and then, a year later, the Tosa breed, the Dogo Argentino, and the Fila were all banned as well. What is particularly bizarre about this is that at the time that these other breeds were banned, the Tosa was represented in England by a grand total of one animal, this the most mild-mannered bitch I have ever witnessed in any breed and I'm not sure that either the Dogo or the Fila were represented at all, throughout the United Kingdom. They were simply banned because these people scare so incredibly easily and relinquish their rights even more easily.

Areas of Germany and, I believe, Holland and Scandinavia as well have banned Pit Bulls. Areas of France are considering similar legislation, as are parts of the Orient, Australia, and elsewhere. Only yesterday, I got an e-mail informing me that the Pit Bull breed had just been totally banned in Sweden, of all places! It wouldn't seem possible that Pit Bulls could have presented such a problem in Sweden that the government there would have seen it as being necessary to pass a law against them, but apparently this law now exists. And here I am, living in America, suggesting that purebred enthusiasts in other countries might be our only hope of preserving these fine dogs in any meaningful form.

No, I was wrong. It's here that these dogs will continue to exist, if they are to continue to exist. It's we Americans who will have to get our law making under control and learn how to say "NO!" to special-interest groups like the "ban-the-Pit-Bullers" and others if the average person's basic rights are to be preserved. I'll tell you, while I am generally suspicious of those who have an interest in politics, I am downright fearful of those among us who let others do the decision making for us, because this is what "the others" do. We are just going to have to put our collective foot down and say "NO!" when we hear these crazy laws being proposed— that's all. We'll have to vote the "let's pass more laws" bums out.

A good American Bulldog with a good American
name: this is Apache from Austria.

This muscular Pit Bull won a specialty show
in Germany in 1994.

Q. What do you feed your dogs?

A. One of the many good things about having one (or two) dogs is that I can afford to feed them whatever I want to. I feed a top-shelf dry food and I supplement this food with table scraps. If you are going to feed as I do, be sure that the animal eats its dry food before you allow it any table scraps or you will soon have a dog that will only eat table scraps.

Q. Should I have my dog professionally trained?

A. It is my belief that if you need to have your dog professionally trained, you probably shouldn't have a dog in the first place. Dog trainers, by and large, are born, they are not made. If you intend to own a "tough dog," you had better be a person who dominates the dog every minute of every day, not by extending an effort in this direction, but rather by simply being the dominant member of the man and dog duo. This is not to say that you shouldn't have a basic understanding of "dog psychology," no matter how "dominant" an individual you may be. Dogs don't think like people do. They do things that are often difficult to understand, unless you have been around enough dogs to have seen it all. It will not help you, however, to have your dog shipped out to a trainer, even if the trainer is someone who does understand dogs, and have it shipped back "trained." The dog will simply revert to what it would have been anyway as soon as it learns that it cannot take direction from you.

Personally, I think dogs are too popular. I think there are far more dogs owned than should be owned. I think that before you get a dog, you had better know that you want a dog and that you are able to cope with having a dog around all the time. Let me tell you, back in the days when no one knew what a Pit Bull was, it was much easier to own a Pit Bull than it is now. People used to stop me on the street and ask me if my Pit Bull wasn't "the same kind of dog they had in the Our Gang comedy series. Now people cross the street when they see a Pit Bull coming in their direction. We were all much better off before.

Q. Why are the pictures in your first book so bad? (I've been asked this question many times, most recently by Hyungwon Kang, a Jindo breeder and a professional staff photographer employed by the *L.A. Times.*)
A. The photographs in my first book aren't bad at all. They're all great! They may not be what someone with an eye for photography would consider to be an artistic success, but they did give my readers their first peek at a category of dogs they knew nothing about.

These three Korean Jindos were photographed by Hyungwon Kang of the *L.A. Times*. Thanks to his generosity and the cooperation of other great dog photographers around the world, this book has great pictures of great dogs.

In order to appreciate those photographs as I did when I first obtained them, you need to be hungry for new information. Remember, in spite of the fact that all kinds of people will tell you that they were breeding Tosas, American Bulldogs, etc., a year or more before my book was published, the truth of the matter is that virtually no one in the United States was breeding these dogs, virtually no one in the United States had any of these dogs, and virtually no one in the United States had ever heard of these dogs. Should you doubt this, call one of the major dog magazines and ask them to send you a copy of any issue of their magazine dating to the year before my book came out. Believe it or not, in spite of the lofty claims of so many modern breeders, there wasn't one ad for the American Bulldog, the Tosa, the Bordeaux

Dogue or others. Not one! Virtually everyone who became interested in these breeds did so as a result of reading that book and seeing those pictures. Few will admit it though, and many simply don't realize that this is the case.

Remember too that when I collected those pictures, I did so by calling dogmen, talking dogs, and getting them to send me their own snapshots of their dogs. I didn't send some professional photographer out to take the pictures for me. The idea was to impress people by providing new information, not by appealing to their artistic nature.

Q. How do you break up a fight between a Pit Bull and another dog?

A. This is a good question made especially valuable by the great amount of misinformation provided in response to it elsewhere. By way of answering it here, let me quote from a lengthy posting on this subject which was offered to a small group of Pit Bull Terrier enthusiasts on the Internet. The following was posted by Mikel Bartol and I think it answers the question well.

"Breaking sticks, what they are and how do they work?"

I'm going to preface this tutorial with a little information on my background in order to establish a little credibility. Don't worry, I'll keep it short and to the point.

In the early 1970s I worked as a trainer/agitator for Aztek kennels in El Paso, Texas, followed by various other kennels over the course of about 15 years. A lot of my work revolved around training dogs to be aggressive toward humans via the avenue of "protection work." "Compound dogs" for car lots to "sentry dogs" for the military. It afforded me exposure to all kinds of breeds and personalities in the canine world. Concurrent to this, I had a fascination with the American Pit Bull Terrier. Okay, the stage is set. You now know why I was exposed to conditions that were just right for accidental fights.

Over the years I've seen so many kennel fights I couldn't possibly count them. In the early years I saw just about every technique known to man used to stop a dog fight. Some of them are as follows:'

lifting and spreading the rear legs
water dousing
strangulation
electric shocks
beating the dog with whatever was handy
praying to God And so on, and so on...

In the late 1970s through the late 1980s I lived down the street from one of the most famous APBT breeders of all time, the late Howard Heinzl. Those of you familiar with the breed will immediately recognize his name. It was he who first showed me the use of breaking sticks, other folks call them parting sticks. Through repeated exposure to the breed you will eventually witness them in a fight and it was one of these occasions on which I was introduced to the breaking stick. I was visiting Howard one day when one of his bitches (in heat) got out of her kennel, ran over to one of the other bitches in Howard's yard and they started to fight. Howard calmly walked into the house, came out with what looked like a contoured door stop, and tossed it to me. I said, "What the heck is this thing?" (He had one too.) He said "It's a breaking stick" and that I should quit talking and get my tail over to where the two bitches were trying to kill each other. With a 5-second tutorial from Howard, I was able to help him break the dogs apart

in about 10 or 15 seconds and that, my friends, is considered slow\
I became a believer from that point on.

THE FIGHT

There comes a time in every dog's life when they will get into some sort of a scrap, be it a small terrier or a powerful APBT. Those of you who frequent dog shows where the APBT is shown will no doubt eventually be witness to dogs getting loose and starting a fight. So, what happens when they are serious? Well, each dog will bite the other, take hold and start to shake its head in the interest of punishing its opponent. It is so serious that in most cases, nothing you do will cause the dog/bitch to give up that precious hold. Nothing! Choking, shocking, etc...It just doesn't matter.

BREAKING/PARTING STICKS

It is a very hard piece of wood or some other material suitable for the purpose of spreading a dog's jaws apart. It is usually about five to eight inches in length, wedge shaped and contoured to prevent injury to the dog's lips. Its width is about one to two inches.

When looking in your dog's mouth, notice a gap where the teeth do not meet. This premolar area is why the breaking stick is so effective.

THE TECHNIQUE

Okay. Imagine two dogs engaged in serious combat and each one has a very good hold on the other. Now, I am assuming there are two of you and you are both right-handed.

STEP 1

Walk over to the dogs and, as simultaneously as possible, step over, straddle and then lock your legs around the dog's hips just in front of the hindquarters. Make sure your legs are locked securely around the dogs.

STEP 2

With your free (left) hand, grab a handful of skin from the back (nape) of the neck and pull upward as if you are a mother canine picking up a young puppy. A strong grip on the skin is needed here. We are accomplishing two things: One is to neutralize the mobility of the dog by locking our legs around its hips, and the other is to neutralize mobility of the front torso by way of a skin hold on the back of the dog's neck.

(Before I continue with Step 3, let's review what has now happened. Not wanting to let go, the dogs are still holding on to each other and each handler has his dog in a tight leg squeeze just in front of the stifle or hindquarters while at the same time holding the dog's front section by way of skin on the back of the dog's neck.)

STEP 3

Each handler inserts his breaking stick in the premolar area where the gap is found. Sometimes you need to work the stick just a bit if your dog is biting very hard. The stick should be inserted from one half inch to one and one half inches into the dog's mouth.

STEP 4

Now, as if you're twisting the throttle of a motorcycle, so you must twist the breaking stick. This is the action that spreads the

Yikes! (Now let's re-read that answer.)

dog's jaws far enough apart so that you can now pull back with the other hand. *Voila!* The dog is off! I also like to use my legs for those big dogs when pulling them off.

IT'S THAT SIMPLE.

The above is useful information for those who find themselves in a position in which your dog is locked on to another dog and you have no idea how you are going to rectify this situation. I can tell you one thing from personal experience. If you think the old "pepper spray" method is going to work, you will undoubtedly be very surprised some day. I tried this once, and to my amazement, the spray, that was made to immobilize a man instantly, had no effect upon the dog I blasted at all. My dog made quite an "impression" upon this loose attacking dog, however.

An appealing American Bulldog, this is Bill Hines's
Vicky, a Williamson-line daughter of China Doll.

*Q. If there were so few American Bulldogs before you began to
write articles about them for dog magazines, and before you
wrote your book, how did you first become interested in the breed?*
(This question comes to me fairly often, most recently from
Sammy Holloway of Landers, California.)

A. I knew of "the Bulldog" long before I began to make a
study of the breed. You will find pictures of an American
Bulldog that belonged to my mother around 1920 or so
in this book. She spoke of the breed she called simply "the
Bulldog" often, but as is so often the case, as children, we
don't listen carefully enough to our parents.

It wasn't until 1975, while living in Tennessee, that a
friend began to talk to me about a friend of hers who kept
white Bulldogs, but not showy-type Bulldogs or Pit Bulls.

At first it didn't even register that this was the same breed my mother had spoken about so often. A few years later, and I don't remember exactly how, I came across an ad for these dogs in the old ARF pulp-paper stockman's magazine out of Quinlan, Texas, and I picked up the phone and called a few breeders. Realizing how few and unknown these dogs and breeders were, I decided to write an article on them for *Dog World* magazine. The breed took off from there.

Q . *Why did you feature Johnson dogs in your first book?* (Again, this question comes to me, every now and then, but most recently it came from Sammy Holloway of Landers, California.)

A. Listen, and listen good, because this is an important part of American Bulldog history and unless you learn it now, it may be lost forever because I'm getting tired of saying it.

This question worries me because it demonstrates to me just how little people understand about where the American Bulldog was during the late 1970s and very early 1980s. For all practical purposes, there were none! There were only a few breeders producing these white bully stockdogs. Only three or four made any effort to present these dogs as a saleable item. The few who did offer pups for sale did so through the ARF stockman's magazine and they offered them to stockmen only. That was it!

Say what you will about Johnson, the fact remains that had it not been for his efforts to offer Bulldogs for sale to others, it is very possible that the American Bulldog would be extinct as a breed by now. As popular as this breed has become today, there was this period during which there was virtually no interest in the few Bulldogs that were left, and Johnson got the breed over that hump. There were two or three others too, most notable among them being Alan Scott of Alabama, but to deny Johnson his due is to misunderstand the history of this breed.

Regardless of what you think of what Johnson has done in recent years, we must give credit where credit is due or we diminish ourselves. When I first began to call him to talk

"OK, OK, enough about the American Bulldog... let's get on with it," yawns Chuck Rock.

about Bulldogs and to ask for pictures to use in publication, Johnson gave me the time I needed and provided the photographs I needed to communicate to others what he and a few others were doing. We shouldn't lose the details of this bit of American Bulldog history.

The Mind
of a Fighting Dog

I t has been said, time and time again, by numerous sources, some of which are commonly viewed as being authoritative, that fighting dogs are, by nature, stupid as compared to other dogs. They conclude that this stupidity is evident in their willingness to fight to the death if need be, in the face of overwhelming odds. One fairly recent reference to this kind of supposed stupidity in dogs can be found in the highly acclaimed book by Stanley Coren entitled *The Intelligence of Dogs* (The Free Press, Macmillan, Inc. 1994). On pages 13 and 14 of this book, Coren speaks of the Dandie Dinmont Terrier and of the courage and tenacity this breed demonstrates when it goes to ground to fight a fox that will weigh roughly the same as the dog, or when it takes on a badger or an otter weighing three times its size. Of these encounters Coren says, "While one might be impressed by the courage shown, one might also feel that a more intelligent dog would simply say (figuratively) this is too dangerous. I'm going to pass this up. This otter has done me no harm."

Personally, I do not feel that intelligence and tenacity are mutually exclusive. After all, have all the military heroes of history simply been idiots? Is our own "Stormin' Norman" Schwarzkopf simply an imbecile and does this explain his utter determination to defeat the Iraqi Military in the Gulf War? If so, why was there so much talk during that war about the fact that this man had an IQ in the 170s, which would undoubtedly rank him somewhere around the 99.99th percentile among humans with regard to his intelligence? And how about "old" George Foreman? Have you ever heard him speak on "Charlie Rose" or elsewhere? This is no dope, folks.

No, to say that dogs willing to accept any challenge are obviously brainless, strikes me as being thoughtlessly simplistic. These dogs may be more easily offended than you and I. They may be less willing to accept defeat than you and I. And they may, like all dogs, be less capable of finding other avenues to ascertain the defeat of an opponent than you and I. Nonetheless this "Damn the torpedoes! Full speed ahead!" attitude of the fighting dogs, the attribute we call "gameness," is explained by recognizing their courage, not their stupidity.

As a matter of fact, I find many of the fighting dogs to be extremely intelligent. Like people, within any breed some representatives will be more intelligent than others, but for the most part, these are fairly smart dogs. Before we can

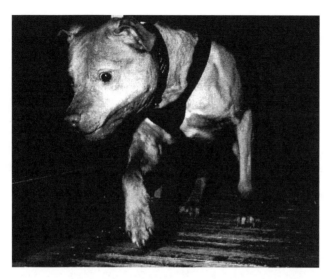

They call him Blinky. Working out on a treadmill in Germany.

agree that any breed is "smart" however, it's important that we are all evaluating the same characteristics in making our determination. Many base their opinion that a particular breed of dog is smart or stupid upon that breed's willingness to respond to human commands. I don't. I may judge a breed's value to me upon its willingness and ability to respond to my commands, but I feel that I have met many a smart dog that simply couldn't care less what I wanted it to do.

The Akita is a breed that is notorious for ignoring human commands, for example. Many Akita owners will disagree with this assessment of the breed, but it has been my experience that many Akita owners came to the breed from other Northern breeds, such as the Malamute or the Husky. Northern breeds, in general, are not good at obeying commands from humans, but among these breeds the Akita is often a bit more willing than others, hence the reputation of being "smart" among "Akita people." I have yet to meet an Akita owner who came to the breed after having owned Dobermans (not a fighting breed) who will tell you that the Akita is an obedient dog. I've never felt that this unwillingness to take orders indicated that the Akita is stupider than other dogs, however. My hunch is, in fact, that if you were to air lift an Akita and a Doberman into a remote wilderness area, drop the dogs there and leave them to fend for themselves for a year, it would be the Akita that would immediately adapt and survive, while the Doberman might not fare very well at all.

A thoughtful, noble Pit Bull from Germany.

Furthermore, I'd bet that a Malamute would adapt most easily of all and take to the wild like it had been born there, while the Doberman or the Pit Bull would sit in the cold and wonder what to do first.

Although I've never had any reason to view any of the fighting breeds as being less intelligent than other dogs, it's important for the prospective owner of one of these dogs

Although the Neapolitan Mastiff may not look very
bright, it is one very intelligent breed.

to understand that the fighting breeds, as a category, do not think alike. Their "personalities" are not the same from breed to breed. We'll discuss the particular characteristics of each of the fighting breeds later, but for the time being, suffice it to say that the owner of a Bull Terrier might well find the Pit Bull or the Neapolitan Mastiff to be too "serious" a dog. Fanciers of any of these breeds would likely find the Akita or the Jindo to be too unresponsive. The owner of a Bordeaux Dogue might well find the Staffordshire Bull Terrier to be far too animated for a house pet, while the owner of the Staff

Bull might find the Bordeaux Dogue to be less playful than he would like.

There are important similarities among the fighting breeds, however. The most important of these similarities is the fact that all of these are "serious" dogs. This is to say that all tend to make a poor choice for first time dog owners. They are "dominant" dogs that require an experienced owner in order to be dominated themselves. They are often aggressive around other dogs and can make a novice owner's neighbors really mad in the event that the novice owner's dog gets out, unattended, at any point.

Worst of all, these dogs, like many breeds of dogs, can sometimes be a liability. This is especially so when the dog finds itself in the hands of a novice dog owner. To avoid giving the impression here that I am admitting to anyone that the fighting breeds are especially dangerous, let me state very firmly and in no uncertain terms, that the kind of atavistic prey drive that one sometimes finds in a functionally capable Bulldog, is normally even more evident in a Whippet, in many Greyhounds, and in countless other breeds. As I said earlier, as a general statement, I think too many people own too many dogs and that the world of dogs, as well as the world of human beings, would be far better off if people took on the responsibility of dog ownership in a much less impulsive and far more responsible manner.

Puppyhood is no worse for the owner of one of the fighting breeds than it is for any other dog owner. As a rule, all of these dogs housebreak without any particular difficulty. Because of the strength and the dominant character of these dogs, it is very important to establish the pecking order of the household early on and not to tolerate any rough stuff

A crossbred Neo-Pit Bull from Germany that you
might call a Bandog.

on the part of the dog from the first day you bring the dog
home. Rough games, like tug-o-war with a rag, are generally
not a good idea. Running to the front door and putting up
a fuss in order to teach the dog to be protective of the house
is not a good idea, unless the person doing the teaching has
had experience in this area. These are naturally protective
dogs and encouraging them to be protective when the dog is
young can lead to the development an overly territorial dog.
The bottom line here is that unless you know what you're
doing before you bring one of these dogs home, this would
be a poor place to begin your experience as a protection dog
trainer. If you like these dogs but you are unsure of your

ability to train a dog properly, a good, basic, obedience class is probably a good idea.

Always keep in mind when adding one of these dogs, or any large, powerful dog to your family, that any chain is only as strong as its weakest link. While you might be perfectly capable of dominating and controlling your dog, your two-year-old might not be. At the first indication that there is any disrespect on the part of the dog for any family member, accept the fact that you have a problem and separate your dog from your family as soon as possible. In any instance of a serious dog bite that I have ever heard of, all the warning signs had made themselves readily apparent well in advance of the problem having arisen, and they went unheeded.

Finally, "chill out" when you bring one of these dogs home as a puppy. Don't let the fact that you have "a really tough dog" go to your head. These dogs, like so many other dogs, enjoy family life. They like being treated like "the family dog." They like to have their own, little, warm spot on the rug.

They like to get their bellies rubbed. They like to play with kids and adults alike. They thrive upon affection, just like any other dog. Your primary reason for getting one of these dogs should always be that you simply want to have a dog in your life. If you aren't a fan of dog ownership generally, you will undoubtedly not enjoy owning one of these dogs. If you find that your dog's affectionate nature disappoints you, you will end up living with an unhappy dog. These dogs don't want to be someone's hobby. They want to be an addition to your family. Get one only if you are looking for this kind of addition to your family.

Tough Guy's Evita, bred and owned by Guenther Haas of Austria, enjoying playtime in the snow.

Organized Dogfighting Today

The underground activity of organized dogfighting is probably more popular and more widespread than ever. This would seem to be an unlikely development in view of the fact that since the publication of my first book, organized dogfighting has been declared a felony in the United States, and laws in other countries have been enacted to ban the keeping of Pit Bull Terriers. In spite of the risk of arrest, dog fighters throughout the United States not only continue to fight Pit Bulls, but they have added other breeds to their repertoire of fighting dogs. Today, along with the Pit Bull, the American Bulldog is more actively fought than ever before. The Japanese Tosa is occasionally matched by

American pit fighters, and a variety of other breeds have been tried against the traditional fighting dogs.

Throughout the United States dogfighting is no longer the sport of an underground fighting fraternity alone. Serious, highly organized dog fighters still exist, matching primarily Pit Bulls to Pit Bulls, or American Bulldogs to other American Bulldogs. Also, there is a huge wave of less organized, less knowledgeable dog fighters participating in what they think is "dogfighting." These are men, often more accurately "boys," who match "front running" dogs, that are larger, heavier boned, more aggressive, and more impressive to look at on the street—though less tenacious or impressive to watch in a dog pit for more than half an hour.

The kind of match that this new crop of Pit Bull fighter participates in repulses many old-time dogmen for two reasons. The first reason is that these matches prove nothing. These dogs fight ferociously for a short period of time and then they quit. Their gameness is rarely seriously tested. The dogs are bred to be hard and fast, but the definitive quality of gameness is not selected for in these dogs. The second reason is that these matches are inordinately brutal. They are often conducted right out on the street with no meaningful training or schooling behind the dogs being matched. Also, there is little veterinary experience available to save the dogs that are hurt in these matches. Some may find it hard to believe that serious pit fighters tend to view their dogs, and their opponents' dogs, with respect and view this manner of brutal activity to be unworthy of their breed.

These matches are numerous and the number of people and dogs participating in them are tremendous. These days it seems that everyone owns a Pit Bull. Once I could spend

A fine search and rescue American Staffordshire
Terrier, this is Schaller's Champ, living and working
in Germany.

literally years walking the streets of New York City without ever seeing another Pit Bull; today I see a Pit Bull on virtually every street corner.

This popularity has not been good for the breed. The very look of the breed, on the whole, has changed over a few, short years, to take on the appearance that the novice puppy buyer demanded. Today the breed looks big and it looks mean. When there were fewer dogs and when the breed, on the whole, was a tougher breed than it is now, the dogs looked smaller and more comical. This is an interesting paradox.

The good dogs are still out there. They remain in demand only by those who are less interested with form than they are with function. Dedicated pit fighting men still talk of the dogs of the 1970s and '80s and recall their pedigrees better than they do their own genetic backgrounds. They know what modern day dogs the dogs of yesterday have given rise to.

They match these dogs, they report the matches participated in by these dogs, and they breed game dogs, just as they did before the breed exploded in popularity.

This isn't the only country in which dogfighting is being conducted on a serious level. Throughout the United Kingdom, Pit Bulls were game tested and matched just as they are here until an act of Parliament banned the breed altogether. What Parliament could not do was to ban the Staffordshire Bull Terrier and the Bull Terrier as well, so rather than stop matching dogs, British dogmen just switched breeds. Additionally, many British dogmen simply changed the name of their breed from American Pit Bull Terrier to Staffordshire Bull Terrier and began breeding game-bred, Pit Bull lines into their Staff Bulls. One would think that Parliament would have known better than to have not seen this happening. Today the sport of matching good game-bred Staff Bulls is alive and well throughout the United Kingdom.

With a bone to pick, this is Gorgona Taiss owned by Michael Egorov of St. Petersburg, Russia, where the Bull Terrier is very popular.

76

As many of the photographs in this book will demonstrate, well-bred American Pit Bull Terriers have found a great following throughout much of Europe. It was in the Netherlands where European dogmen first began to match very game Pit Bulls in a serious effort to re-establish this sport in Europe during modern times, but since then, the activity has spread like wildfire throughout Europe, panicked efforts on the part of legislators everywhere to ban the ownership of these dogs notwithstanding. The same situation exists throughout Asia too, and I am often amazed by the detailed knowledge of pedigrees demonstrated by Chinese, Japanese, Russian, etc., dogmen who write me from time to time. It's difficult to imagine that this sport could have gotten so big so fast.

The Pit Bull is not the only breed of interest to dogfighting men throughout the world. In Japan, Tosa matches continue to maintain a large following, these matches ranging in style from the Sumo-like pushing matches that may be seen in touristy places like the Tosatoken Fighting Center in Kochi, to brutal, hard-fought matches outdoors in backyards, gas stations, and elsewhere throughout Japan. Fighting Tosa dogs is not an activity conducted in Japan alone. The Tosa dog has become very popular among pit men in Korea, Taiwan and elsewhere in Asia, and to a lesser extent, in Hawaii. It is interesting to note that in places like Korea and Taiwan, where good game-bred, American Pit Bull Terriers and even a number of good American Bulldogs have become established, Tosa fighting has not been displaced. If the Tosa dog was as useless a fighter as many American dogmen would have us believe, why is there still interest in this breed where the Pit Bull has established a stronghold?

Jindo fighting continues in Korea as well. Unlike the Jindo Dogs that are being brought to this country by serious, Korean-American Jindo enthusiasts, however, the Jindos being selected by today's dog fighter in Korea is a crossbred dog. Both Tosa and Pit Bull have found their way into fighting Jindo lines in the Jindo's native land. There is some speculation that fighting Jindos have become established in the United States at this point as well, and though evidence does point in this direction, I have not been taken into anyone's confidence and so cannot comment upon this with any degree of authority.

On the Spanish Island of Gran Canaria, situated off the coast of North Africa, of all the unlikely places, the sport of dogfighting is not only alive and well but the breed employed in this activity is an extremely impressive one of native development. On a recent trip to the Canary Islands I sat and chatted with dogmen at length and I can assure you that these guys are as knowledgeable about the fighting breeds of the world as any dog enthusiasts anywhere. They import dogs from all over the world, they game test dogs, and they occasionally use foreign breeds in their own breeding projects. But the goal of their breeding project is to continue to improve the breed known as the Perro de Presa Canario, or the native Canary Dog. Who would have thought it?

Throughout the United States, and throughout much of the world, the American Bulldog has exploded in popularity. The dogs being called American Bulldogs range in type and in genetic backgrounds from huge, sloppy, useless, St. Bernard and Dogue de Bordeaux mutts, to fine, athletic, impressive, catch and fighting dogs. Many serious dogmen are matching their American Bulldogs today in matches that

This 13-month-old Bordeaux pup gives a half-hearted warning to the photographer. Owner, Gerry Pleasant.

are as expertly conducted as any Pit Bull match ever. These dogs are much bigger than the game-bred Pit Bull, and they don't generally fight as long as a Pit Bull can, but they are hard biting dogs and they do damage to their opponents quickly.

So, the sport of organized dogfighting has not gone away in recent years. If anything, it has grown beyond anyone's expectations in size and in scope. This is an activity which, like it or not, pass laws against it or not, has been around for a very long time, and it is becoming ever increasingly clear to me that it will never go away. I think this is an activity that mankind will always know.

Where Did All These Bulldogs Come From?

Relax. This is not going to be a chapter about history. One of the many things I learned from having had my first book published is that if you say anything in a chapter heading indicating that the chapter is going to be about history, nobody reads the chapter. I'll tell you what though, having written the chapter on the history of dogfighting in my first book and having had so few comments on it was a frustrating experience. I liked that chapter. I thought it was a well-thought-out chapter. I thought, and I still think, that in addition to having discussed a few now popular breeds for the first time, anywhere, that the chapter on the history of the bulldog was a real contribution to purebred history. As I said, the book is still available and anyone who wants to read what I said about where I think the bulldog came from can secure a copy of that book and read that chapter. I really wish you would because it's time that we begin to realize that the bulldog of old, and all of the bulldog breeds of today, are not what we think they are. They are not what purebred-dog literature and purebred historians would have us think they are. They are something else altogether.

On a very simple, straightforward level, let me offer you the following facts and make the following case. Brachycephalism (a head as broad as it is long) in dogs is a characteristic that is very difficult to develop and to maintain. This characteristic is typical of the bull breeds and of the small toy Asian breeds. The British are commonly credited with having developed the bulldog, and so, when we consider the history of all of today's bulldog related breeds, we immediately credit the British with having begun the whole thing.

But at the time that we first see the bulldog referred to in English literature (or anywhere) brachycephalism did not exist in English dogs. Indeed, brachycephalism did not exist in Western European breeds. This unusual characteristic existed only in Asian (originally and primarily Chinese) breeds (the "sleeve dogs" such as today's Pekingese, etc.). No Western European breeds exhibited the characteristic of brachycephalism prior to the first mention of bulldogs in the literature. The literature would have us believe that brachycephalism just showed up overnight. Any two-bit dog breeder can tell you that brachycephalism doesn't just show up overnight. You've got to work for it.

So how did brachycephalic dogs get from Asia to England? Mariners brought them, that's how. This is what

Two Tough Guys: American Staffordshire Terriers
from Austria. Owner, Guenther Haas.

mariners do. My father, Anton Semencic of Dalmatia, was a mariner. He was a merchant marine all of his working life and he told me many stories of the dogs that seamen would take on as ship's mascots. His most interesting dog stories were of one ship's Bull Terrier and another ship's Tosa. Tough guys often like tough dogs. It's as simple as that.

We know that when Western European trade with Asia was first established, one of the first things brought to Asia was Western European terriers. Guess when brachycephalic dogs are first discussed in the literature of Western Europe? Much more than coincidentally, it was at the same time that trade relations were first established between Western Europe and Asia. For the details of all of this, see my first book *The World Of Fighting Dogs* or ask *Dog World* magazine for reprints of my articles in back issues. The details and the timeframes are discussed there.

But why brachycephalism? Why did the Chinese want to introduce this unusual, grotesque feature to their dogs? Again, much more than coincidentally, other things were going on in China at the time that brachycephalism was developed in dogs. For one thing, the art of Bonsai (not originally a Japanese art but rather a Chinese art) was being developed. Do you know it? I took a class in Bonsai once and I practice it, minimally, now. Bonsai is to trees what the Pekingese is to dogs. Bonsai is the art of stunting otherwise huge trees so that they can be kept in a small pot. They can grow for about the normal life of a tree this way. The point here is that at the same time that Chinese sedentary farmers were first developing the art of Bonsai, they were also developing the art of introducing brachycephalism in dogs. They were playing with stunting nature. But why? What would have motivated these people to play with the newly developed art of stunting nature?

Champion Tosa owned by Mr. Yokoshima of Japan.

Yet again, much more than coincidentally, at precisely the time when these Chinese, sedentary farmers were developing the arts of Bonsai and brachycephalism in dogs, they were being raided by Mongol Warriors. These Mongols were fierce, scary people who raided, raped, killed, stole, and generally pillaged. They could come at any time and they could impose upon these sedentary Chinese farmers, horrible memories that would last a lifetime. While these ancient forms of art were being developed, this is what was going on in these people's lives. The Great Wall of China was constructed to protect these Chinese agriculturists from these raiding, Mongol, people!

Guess what historians describe these raiding Mongols as looking like. The Mongols are described by prominent historians as having been a short, stout, large-headed, brachycephalic people with short arms and legs. They rode horses that were also short and stout with large, wide heads. Folks, here is the influential power that caused these sedentary Chinese farmers to be thinking about thick, brachycephalic forms of nature. This influence gave rise to the development of brachycephalic dogs which happened to appear in Western Europe at precisely the time when brachycephalism first occurs there, in the form of our early bulldog.

Finally, and because I am utterly absent minded and so I can't prove this, we have to wonder why those Western Europeans who first developed the Bulldog would have been interested in "sleeve dogs." It's a valid question. If one wants to develop the world's greatest fighting dog, why does one focus on a sleeve dog as the progenitor of the fighting dog line? I'll tell you what my theory is. I'll tell you how I can semi-substantiate my theory, and I will tell you that what I want to come along very much is some person from China, who will help me substantiate this theory by referring to the old literature and the old art work. You guys write me letters to ask about Pit Bull bloodlines and other stuff all the time. Surely you can concentrate your efforts on this question and help me prove that it was your ancestors who gave rise to the bulldog.

My theory is that what survives of ancient Asian brachycephalic dogs today is the pet sleeve dog, but that in fact what existed once, what was originally transported to Western Europe, and that gave rise to the Bulldog was a medium-sized, fierce-fighting, brachycephalic bulldog. I thought this was true, I proved it to myself, and then I lost the evidence because I am absent minded. I found the evidence by setting out to look for it. I went to the Metropolitan Museum of Art in New York (I've looked elsewhere too, including the Louvre) and finally found a book on Chinese art that contained a picture of a painting that proved that my theory was correct, to me anyway.

In the painting from China I found depicted a man holding a chain to which was attached the most ferocious-looking bulldog I have ever seen. It was one of these Chinese paintings which leads the viewer uncertain as to whether he or she had been looking at the depiction of a fierce dog or perhaps, instead, the depiction of one of the old Chinese lions. This one was a dog. I was so surprised by having finally found what I had been looking for so intently that I saw no need to copy the source down. I felt certain, at the time, that I'd

Chinese Shar-Pei from the Netherlands. The author has seen some nasty Shar-Pei in the past, though the show ring has done a good job of weeding out nasty dispositons.

never forget it. Guess what happened. Right. I completely forgot the source and I have been unable to find it again. It's out there though and it makes my case, even though as far as I am concerned, my case is made without the picture. I certainly welcome anyone, anywhere, to help me in this endeavor, but again, the important thing to remember is that there was no brachycephalism in Western Europe at the time that the Bulldog suddenly appears in history books. There were brachycephalic dogs in Asia at this time. Again, at the time that brachycephalism appears in Western Europe, trade relations began, via merchant seamen, between Western Europeans and Asians. Why have we dog historians not seen that brachycephalism was brought to Europe from Asia and not developed in Europe before?

I promised you at the beginning of this chapter that this would not be a discussion of history and I guess it's fairly obvious by now that I lied about that. You must admit that I have not piled on a million details (exact dates, precise locations of ports of call, names of historians who refer to Mongols as having been brachycephalic, etc.). All of these have been published by me, either in my first book or in articles published years ago, however, and I would advise anyone who is interested in reading these to go back into the literature and find it. Better still, go to history books that are not about dogs and prove all of this to yourselves. Once this has been done, let's give all this other dog history, i.e., 'The Bulldog is a breed of purely British origin..." a rest and begin to talk about and to understand where these dogs actually came from. If I can prompt you to do this, I'll feel like I've done something.

Zeke, a five-year-old, 75-pound male Olde English Bulldogge, became the foundation stud for Mike Walz. This Bulldogge is described as very tough.

The loyal Hachiko, the famous Akita tribute at the Shibuya station in Toyko. As the story goes, Hachiko accompanied his owner to the station every day on the way to work, and then would return to meet his master at day's end. One day the master died suddenly while at work. The Akita waited at the station until midnight and returned every evening to wait for his master for the next nine years. Finally Hachiko succumbed to old age. True or not, something motivated the people of Tokyo to erect this tribute to the loyal Hachiko. Photograph courtesy of Redmond Young.

AKITA

The Akita is a fighting dog from Japan. Its usefulness as a fighting breed has long since been superseded by the appearance of the Tosatoken or Tosa dog, also of Japan, but the Akita, like so many other fighting breeds, is of purely, or at least largely, gladiator heritage. To say this with such certainty is to say a mouthful, to be sure, because so many Akita fanciers would deny that this is so. The reason for this denial of the fighting heritage of the Akita is that most Akita fanciers feel that the association with its pit fighting past is a negative association that can only serve to get the Akita in trouble with lawmakers and so it is best forgotten. Maybe five percent of these fanciers have actually done their homework, realized what the truth of the Akita is, and opted to present the breed as a bear-hunting dog instead (which it also is, by the way). The remaining 95 percent haven't got a clue what the Akita is but insist that it is not a breed of gladiator heritage for no better reason than that they feel they know this, intuitively. They have heard from others that it is not a fighting dog and because they don't want it to be a fighting dog, they insist that these others are right and that I am wrong. So be it.

In *The World of Fighting Dogs* I explained why I felt the Akita was a dog of fighting heritage. I am making a very conscious, concerted effort not to repeat myself here, no matter how tempting it may get to do so. As such, let's assume that if you are interested in this question you have either read or will read *The World Of Fighting Dogs*. To further my case that the Akita is a fighting breed, let me take the argument one step beyond where I left it in the first book and go on to explain another dilemma that Akita fanciers face.

The classic American-bred Akita, i.e., an Akita of Japanese origin but bred from genetic lines that have been cultivated in the United States so long that they are now distinctly American, and the classic Japanese-bred Akita are very different in appearance and, as a result, do not show well together in the show-ring at all. This is a curious situation. After all, an English-bred Staffordshire Bull Terrier shows just fine against American-bred Staff Bulls. Many other breeds have no problem similar to the one the Akita faces. Why should Japanese and American Akitas look so different?

The answer is that the Akita was first brought to the United States by servicemen who were stationed in Japan during the Second World War. At that time, the Tosa influence upon Akita lines was still quite obvious. The Japanese, being unwilling to totally relegate the traditional fighting dog of Japan to the trash heap (purely from any dog fighter's perspective, mind you) of the hunting fields, bred the more successful fighting dog of Japan, the Tosa, into fighting Akita bloodlines. The upshot of all this cross breeding was that the dogs that did the winning in Japan were the ones with the most Western breeding behind them, i.e., the purely Western Tosas. The Tosa/Akita crosses didn't do well at all, but they did better than pure Akitas.

Because these Tosa-to-Akita crosses were not winning in the Japanese dog pits, and because American servicemen who didn't know any better fell in love with these mostly lupoid Japanese fighting dogs. Japanese dog fighters saw the exodus of American servicemen at the end of the war as a great chance to rid themselves of their Akita/Tosa crosses and to stick with the winning Tosas themselves. The dogs the American servicemen brought back were primarily Akita/Tosa mutts. They were primarily lupoid in appearance but displayed mollosoid physical characteristics as well, including larger heads, bigger bone, larger, more pendulous lips, etc. In the meantime, Japanese dog fighters concentrated their efforts on breeding purely mollosoid (Mastiff/Bulldoglike) dogs, because these were the winning pit dogs, while Japanese Akita show enthusiasts concentrated their efforts upon ridding themselves of everything Western, including the Western European influence upon their formerly purely lupoid Akita dogs.

Herein lies the problem in the Akita show-ring during the latter half of the 20th century. The ideal American Akita show dog still displays the mollosoid features. The Japanese-bred Akita, having been rid of these features, appears small and more fox-like by comparison. To judge these dogs together is to judge apples against oranges.

Don Lee of Honolulu, Hawaii with Mutusu, a fine
Tosa who is now deceased. Compare Mutsu with
some of the big American-style Akitas—you can
really see the influence of the Tosa on American
Akita lines.

Some will argue that all I have managed to do here is to prove that a pure Akita is a lupoid (wolf like) animal and that it is not until Tosa influence was added to Akita lines that the Akita became a fighting dog. In response to this, I have two things to say. The first is that the Tosa has been around since just after the middle of the 1800s. Even if the Akita had never been matched until then, it would be a breed of fighting ancestry by now. The second thing is that when the Japanese first began to cross Western fighting breeds into Japanese bloodlines, the Japanese bloodlines they selected for crossing to Western dogs were obviously their own fighting bloodlines.

Anyone who finds it difficult to believe that early Japanese lupoid dogs were used primarily for fighting, need only to explore the history of the "Jindo" dog of Korea, a purely lupoid, fighting dog as well. Like the Jindo, the Akita was certainly a lupoid, fighting dog before Western influence found its way into Akita lines. It was not a sufficiently competitive fighting dog, hence the crossing of the lupoid lines to the Mollosoid lines, upon the arrival of the Bull and Mastiff breeds to Japan. Interestingly, in recent years, the Korean Jindo has also been crossed to Western fighting breeds to improve its fighting ability and it is the struggle of Jindo "purists" to maintain the purely lupoid Jindo as a Korean National Treasure.

Oddly, this is something that the Japanese know. Japanese dogmen do not deny any of what has been said above, as American Akita fanciers do. Perhaps this is due to the fact that the Akita is so well respected and well established in Japan that Japanese Akita fanciers have no

Trevor Small with one of his Akitas. Trevor likes his Akitas to be tough.

fear of legislation, similar to so much of today's anti-Pit Bull legislation, will ever be passed against the breed there.

Again, I suppose that many American Akita fanciers see what the label "fighting dog" has done for the Pit Bull and feel that they are better off without the same label. To these people I will say that the label "fighting dog" also applies, without dispute, to the Boxer, the Bulldog, the Boston Terrier, etc. and, like the Akita, because these dogs have been found to be non-competitive with the Pit Bull and so non-threatening to society, the label has done them no harm.

Give it up. Admit the history. To deny the facts simply leaves everyone with less information than one needs in order to evaluate the quality of any particular dog. After all, it is only by understanding the history of a breed that we can evaluate living representatives of that breed or understand the reason the written breed standard is what it is. Remember, the breed standard for the Akita clearly calls for a dog that is "Aggressive Toward Other Dogs." Guess why?

As I have already said, the reason that so many Akita breed fanciers disagree with me about the historical background of the Akita has nothing to do with academics, historical reconstruction, etc. I doubt that what I have said here will change any of their minds about what the Akita is. Perhaps, if I have given some of you some useful information, there will be enough pressure put upon Akita breed historians to begin to face the facts about this breed. Then again, perhaps not. But be this all as it may, the Akita is here to stay and worthy of discussion anyway.

I have finally decided that I am not a big fan of the Akita breed. I have to admit that at first, and for a long time, I was

Ch. Tee Jay's Kato Kid, owned by Gina Brischi
Douglas of New York City.

attracted to the breed because of its wonderful appearance.
The Akita, when it is done right, is a magnificent animal.
Its thick bone, big head, tight enough lips, smallish eyes,
beautiful coat, tightly curled tail, etc., will turn most dog
fancier's eyes. A good, thick, male Akita is a really good
looking dog and those who prefer that look in a dog are

This dog demonstrates the postwar American Akita. Compare the heavy bone and mastiff-like appearance to the Akitas you find in Japan today.

bound to take a second look at the Akita, especially in view of the dominant attitude it exudes.

But the bottom line with the Akita is that it isn't a dog that comes when you call it, and I can't stand a dog that doesn't come when you call it. In this respect, the Akita has a great deal in common with other "Northern Breeds," such as the Samoyed, the Husky, the Malamute, etc. These are all

Champion Avalon Flash de Alicia. Photograph
courtesy of Gina Brischi Douglas.

good, thick, strong, "macho" looking dogs that don't come
when they are called. But in this regard, the Akita is better
than the rest. Possibly, if not probably, due to the Western
breed influence in Akita bloodlines, the Akita is a bit more
responsive than other dogs of breeds which look somewhat
like the Akita. When called from afar, a Malamute will totally
ignore its owner. At least an Akita will look back at you to
see who it is ignoring. I guess that's something, anyway, but
for me it isn't enough. I like a dog that does the basic dog
thing. I like a dog that comes when you call it.

Virtually every breed discussed in this book is a loyal,
"stick by your side" dog. A Pit Bull, an American Bull, or a
Neapolitan Mastiff that has been well raised by an owner
will stick by that owner's side through thick and thin. These
are dogs that love their owner and their human family above
all things and they are not the least bit inclined to wander
off. The Bordeaux Dogue, the Staffordshire Bull and others

This is me with the famous statue of the Akita dog "Hachiko." The statue stands in the square in Shibuya, Tokyo, Japan, just outside the Hachiko entrance to Shibuya Station. This is an incredible meeting place for Tokyoites and everyone in Tokyo knows Hachikko and the story of Hachiko which you can find elsewhere by doing a simple search.

are also a loyal, responsive family dog. The Bull Terrier can be stubborn and have a mind of its own, but a well-bred Bull Terrier that has been raised by an experienced dog owner will stick by an owner's side, and when it does dash off it will do so for a short time and because it has been overcome by its playful spirit.

The Akita is different. When an Akita takes off it does so because immediately upon having slipped its lead it was overcome by the call of the wild. This is more of a cat-like breed in this respect, and this quality is something that some dog owners prefer. I don't, and it has been my experience that other "fighting breed" enthusiasts don't like it either. We prefer a dog that is less independent and that bonds closer to its owner and family. The fact that the Akita is unlike these other breeds in this respect is something that prospective dog owners should know or one could be in for quite a disappointment. An unresponsive nature and an unwillingness to do the basic things that many expect of their dog (i.e., respond to commands regularly) is fine if you don't care about responsiveness in a dog, but it can be very frustrating if it was a closely bonded dog that you were looking for.

Having said all of this, let me assure you that I have known Akitas that have done fairly well in the obedience ring. A very experienced trainer with an especially good Akita can put on a fairly impressive show, but the show is always especially impressive because the dog demonstrating its willingness to obey commands is an Akita. The job would always have been easier had the dog been of a more responsive breed.

I have seen very man-aggressive, highly-territorial Akitas. It is not in the breeds nature to be this way. Should you find yourself the owner of such an Akita, its aggressive nature would best be put to use as a guardian of property, as opposed to using it as a personal protection dog. Again, the breed is not responsive enough to human command to work well as a personal protection dog. Personal protection dogs are highly responsive by definition.

The Akita breed has been slandered in dog literature as a poor fighting dog that is less than "game." I'm not sure that I feel this is a fair assessment of the breed as a dog fighter. While it is true that this breed will not go on and on in a "scratching match," one really shouldn't expect this kind of behavior from a dog that possesses so much more of a "wild" spirit than the totally man-made bulldogs do. The toughest animals in nature turn tail and run when they find themselves in trouble. Does it make sense to demean them for it? I don't think so. After all, genetic superiority, as it is defined for everything in nature, depends upon a living thing's ability to survive another day in order to continue to reproduce. The raw power of an Akita is impressive enough without us wondering why it doesn't care to compete in a dogfight according to modern American dog fighter's rules.

My friend Andy's Akita bitch sitting on a bench in New York City's Central Park. Andy LOVES Akitas.

Meet the Korean Jindo. This photograph is by Hyungwon Kang, a great Jindo enthusiast, who expertly captured this little Jindo and a critter that happened by.

JINDO

Indulge me for just a minute, if you will. Do me the favor of trying to appreciate how much effort went into trying to bring some basic information on the Jindo breed to you. Years from now, all the Jindo experts can tell us about how they were breeding the Jindo in America years before this book came out, but at least for now, try to appreciate how many phone calls I've made, how many letters I've sent, how many dog people I have corresponded with, etc., in order to finally learn, and so be able to present, a bit of information on the Jindo breed of Korea. As of right now, very little has been offered in the way of literature in the English language on the Jindo breed.

Since before the publication of my first book, I have been in search of information on the Korean Jindo dog. All I was able to find out was that it was an ancient

Korean dog that was often used for fighting. From conversations I have had with Korean American purebred enthusiasts, I had learned that the Jindo was a "lupoid" (wolf like) dog, but that was about it.

Finally, in 1994, as a result of my posting an open note on the Internet asking for information about the Jindo, I got a response from a Korean-American who owned a Jindo. This guy put me in contact with another Korean-born American guy who worked for the *L.A. Times* and this guy, Hyungwon Kang, was not only a Jindo owner but a real hard-core Jindo enthusiast. Purely by coincidence, three months after Hyungwon and I first began to call each other on the phone to talk about Jindo dogs, I was walking down Duane Street, on Manhattan's Lower East Side, and there before me was a Caucasian guy walking a Jindo puppy!

I didn't know what to say to this Caucasian guy (Chip) at first. I suspected that the dog he was walking was a Jindo, as impossible as this seemed at the time, but I knew that if I walked up to this total stranger and asked him if his dog was a Jindo, he would more than likely think it was weird. So I asked him if it was a Shiba. He stopped and said "No. It's a Korean relative of the Shiba." I said "You mean it is a Jindo?" Let me tell you, we were both pretty surprised, me because I had just seen my first Jindo and him because he had just met an American who knew what a Jindo was. As it turned out, Chip's wife is Korean. The dog they had gotten was partially out of stock from L. A. I put Chip on to Hyungwon in California and faxed him a copy of the breed standard that Hyungwon had sent me.

The Korean Jindo dog got a slow start in the United States, as well as all points elsewhere, outside of Korea, because the

Kang at a year and half old, owned by the author.
He's running around the woods not far from home,
looking for some squirrels to terrorize. Look at the
grin on his face. He's having a ball.

breed has been regarded as a National Treasure in South Korea and, therefore, its exportation has been prohibited by law. With the relocation of many South Koreans to the United States, many Jindo owners, being unwilling to give up their dogs, managed to smuggle their dogs out of their country (by claiming that they were mixed bred "mutts"). Korean Customs Agents, not viewing Jindo smuggling as being a big deal, overlooked the fact that they recognized the dog exported to be purebred. And so, slowly but surely, the foundation breeding stock which was and is to give rise to Jindo dogs in America emigrated from Korea for the first time.

It is important to understand that while it took awhile for the Jindo to make its way out of Korea, it was not so difficult for the Pit Bull to make its way into Korea. As such, the

A one-year-old Jindo puppy owned by John Choi of
San Jose, California.

clash
of the Jindo fighting dog of Korea and the devastating
fighting ability of the American Pit Bull Terrier parallel the
situation that developed between the Akita dog of Japan and
the Western gladiator breeds brought there by mariners of
old. As was the case with the Akita and the Western bull
and mastiff breeds, the Jindo was matched against the Pit
Bull and it lost. The first response of the Korean Jindo dog

There is something in the look of the Jindo dogs that
goes back a long, long way. This primitive spirit is
captured with elegance by photographer
Hungwon Kang.

fighter was to try to increase the fighting ability of the Jindo,
rather than to give up on the traditional fighting breed of
Korea completely. In this spirit, Pit Bulls and Jindo dogs
became crossbred in Korea, and it wasn't long before many
Jindo dogs began to look more like Pit Bull/Jindo crosses
than they did pure Jindo.

But as was the case with the Akita in Japan, it soon
became obvious that the more Pit Bull a Jindo had in it,
the better it could fight, and ultimately a dog that had no
Jindo in it at all was the best fighter of all. The course for the
Korean Jindo breeder and fancier clearly ran in one of two
directions.

Either they could give up on Jindo dog altogether, or they
could learn to appreciate the Jindo for what it was, and for

Jindos are very different from the kind of dogs
the author's been used to.

what it had always been, without worrying about its lack of ability to beat the Pit Bull in the dog pits.

Fortunately, there were enough Korean Jindo breeders who cared more about the breed generally than they did about which breed was better at fighting, and the Jindo survived. Not only did it survive, but many a Jindo breeder decided that as long as fighting was no longer to be a primary concern, they might just as well breed the Jindo "the way it used to be." Instead of selecting Jindo dogs that were more like Pit Bulls, they began to select dogs that were totally unlike Pit Bulls but, instead, were as much like "old style" Jindo dogs as possible. As a result of this basic love of the breed, the Jindo we see today are generally as pure Jindo as the breed has ever been.

I was much impressed by the first Jindo I had ever seen. It was a fine dog to look at, for one thing. It was a foxy-red and white color, much like that of many Shiba-Inu I have seen. Its face and coat also had that heavy boned but sleek Shiba/Akita/Hokkaido-Ken look that so many Americans have come to admire. Additionally, the dog was considerably larger than a Shiba. I am told that a good male will weigh about 45 pounds, or so.

But more than the look of the dog, I was impressed by the dog's attitude and its spirit. It was a very "alive" and alert little dog. It was young, so the outward aggression that often typifies the breed had not yet taken hold. But what impressed me most was that when I put out my hand to pet it, while it didn't object to my violating its space, it didn't welcome me either. Instead, in an interesting response to my display of affection for it, it turned around and licked its master rather than me.

Jindo pups are very alert and not outwardly
aggressive as the adults can be. Like the Shiba and
Akita, Japanese breeds which this Korean spitz
resembles, the Jindo is aloof but not unaffectionate.

Hyungwon of L.A. tells me that among his friends, it
is common to leave one's shoes at the door when visiting
someone else's home. He tells me that one of his Jindo
bitches would always travel with him, wherever he went, and
when he was visiting, the bitch would sit on the shoes he had
left by the door and remain there until it was time to leave.

I am told that like many of the Asian breeds, the Jindo is
an extremely easy dog to housebreak and to train as a house
pet. The primary use of the breed today is the hunting of
small game, such as rabbits and rats, as well as larger game,
such as deer, badger, and even boar, and it is said that this was
the use for which the breed was originally developed, having
been employed as a fighting dog only much later in time,
when its courage and tenacity became commonly exploited.
Maybe so.

Jindo puppy at seven weeks of age, owned by John Choi.
Thanks to Mr. Choi's contacting with Mr. Kang, our Jindo chapter
has many wonderful photographs to share.

In any event, as much as the Jindo is not the kind of dog I normally prefer to own, I find this breed to be so interesting that I could definitely see myself hunting rabbits with one. I suspect that many American purebred enthusiasts will ultimately feel the same way, and that these dogs will grow in popularity quickly throughout the United States and elsewhere. Again, if it's yet another "world's best fighting dog" you are looking for, this isn't it. But if it's a highly spirited, affectionate, if a bit independent, companion and home guardian you are in the market for, this could very well be the choice for you.

In appearance, the Jindo resembles the spitz breeds of Japan, such as the Kochi, Hokkaido or Kai. In Korea, the white or tan Jindos are the most popular, as they are the only colors that are recognized.

One-year-old Jindo owned by John Choi.

BREED STANDARD FOR THE JINDO DOG
OF KOREA

Because of the current lack of information about the Jindo breed outside of Korea, I am offering the following breed standard. This standard was sent to me by Hyungwon Kang of Los Angeles, California. Mr. Kang also wrote this standard.

Origin: For centuries, the Jindo dog, named after Jindo Island in Southwest Korea, was only available on the Island.

Jindo dogs are good rabbit hunters. This particular
Jindo talent persuaded the author to get a Jindo
himself, so he could "scare up a few rabbits."
Captured by Kang on film (and Kang's dog in
real life), this black-tailed jack rabbit is running
somewhere in the American West.

Under Korean national law, the Jindo dog is protected as the 53rd National Monument. Exporting Jindos out of Korea is prohibited; however, Korean-Americans have been bringing Jindo's to America since the mid-1980s.

Description: The Jindo is a medium-sized dog, robust, pleasant and agile in movement. It has the lean body of a marathoner, capable of running extremely long distances and with effortless gait.

Height: Standard height (height at the withers) for dogs: 45-55 cm (18-22 in.); for bitches: 43-52 cm (17-21 in.).

Weight: For dogs: 15-20 kg (33-44 lb.); bitches: 10-15 kg (22-33 lb.)

Ears: Erect, pointed and very mobile.

Tail: There are two types: ring tail, rolled on its back; erect tail, straight up.

Eyes: Gingko nut-shaped, yellowish brown eyes with clear pupils. Jindos with reddish eyes are considered better hunters.

Expression: The Jindo has a friendly, courteous and energetic expression.

Hair: Korean law currently only recognizes white Jindos and tan Jindos, thus they are most popular colors. Some Jindo Island residents have valued black, black/tan and tan/white Jindos for being good hunters over the years.

Personality: Extremely loyal and affectionate toward its master, a clean animal both in its body as well as its habits, very independent, highly intelligent, proud and trainable only by its master. It is an aggressive fighter among dogs. It has an innate sense of direction and is capable of returning home from several hundred miles away.

In appearance, the Jindo resembles the spitz breeds
of Japan, such as the Kochi, Hokkaido or Kai. In
Korea, the white or tan Jindos are the most popular,
as they are the only colors that are recognized.

Uses: The Jindo specializes in hunting deer, wild boar, rabbit, raccoon, and badger, which it can scent several days after they pass. It loves hunting and vast open spaces. When several Jindo are hunting together for a big game such as deer, after capturing the game, one of the Jindos would return to the master to bring him to the location while other Jindos sit and wait by the game. South Korean military authorities use Jindos on military bases where they learn to recognize thousands of personnel at the base and to detect outsiders. Jindos are said to recognize and remember over 30,000 different scents.

A beautiful Jindo pup, bred and photographed by Hungwon Kang.

Here's the author's son Dan with the family Jindo "Kang," named for photographer and breeder Hyungwon Kang. Dan is eight years old here, and Kang is about seven months. Kang is smart and very alert, highly supicious of strangers but exceptionally friendly to family and friends.

Eddie Dombish with a Korean imported Jindo. The author has considered breeding his male to this bitch, since he likes the dog's attitude (although not her ears, which are too long). He rarely breeds dogs—one visit to the humane society will tell you why.

The Jindo has a tendency to roam, typical of the spitz breeds due to their heavy prey drives. The author warns that these dogs "blow" their coats in springtime, and anyone who doesn't like loose hair all over the house may not be well suited to the Jindo. Owner, John Choi.

East West Trading's Taka once visited the Semencic
family's home—the kids just loved him!

TOSA

For many reasons, the Tosa dog of Japan is among the most misunderstood breeds in modern "dogdom." One reason for this misunderstanding is the speed with which it attained notoriety, not only in the United States but throughout the Western world. A decade and a half ago the Tosa was little more than a rumor that few rare breed enthusiasts in the Western world had even heard. Today numerous advertisements appear in American purebred dog magazines for Tosas, clubs have started up in the United States which bring American Tosa owners and enthusiasts together, the story of the Tosa has been told to purebred enthusiasts in Europe, and the breed has even been totally banned, for absolutely no rational reason at all, throughout the United Kingdom! We'll talk about this more in a little while.

In addition to the Tosa's popularity having leapt forward at a speed that is greater than the average dog enthusiasts capacity to understand it (and I don't mean this in a demeaning way at all). This is a very complicated breed. It is complicated because it is a breed that was and is being bred primarily for its functional ability. With regard to its being produced for any reason that would impress the average purebred enthusiast, it is still in its early stages of development as a breed, in spite of the fact that it has existed for more than a century. I warned you that this was going to be complicated, didn't I? Here's what I mean.

The way the average purebred is originally produced is not at all the way a high-quality show dog is produced. Most purebreds are originally produced in order to do one form of work or another, and in order to produce functionally capable dogs, the strategy that is employed is, more or less, the exact opposite of the strategy employed by a breeder who aims to improve the appearance of an already established purebred. The breeder who is breeding dogs for the show-ring, breeds one good looking dog to another in order to create a dog that looks even better than either of the parents involved. Especially in this country, function is totally unimportant, especially in the case of a fighting dog, while form is everything.

When a dog is bred purely for function, form is totally unimportant unless a breeder starts with the idea that function will follow form. This is virtually never the case, for all practical purposes. Breeders of working dogs generally take note that form follows function, but couldn't really care less whether it does or it doesn't. Dogs that are produced in order to accomplish a task are produced with that end in

Steve Ostuni and a nice, black Tosa pup, East West Trading Katsurahama or "The Dog." According to the breeder Steve, this is the first black Tosa born in the States.

mind only. In the case of the fighting dog, winning, according to established fighting rules of the land, is all important. If winning dogs are bred to winning dogs and the offspring resemble large gerbils more than they do the lowliest of show dogs, that's okay because the object of the game is to win and not to look especially good.

In some instances, the general form that will follow function (and we should keep in mind that generally speaking, form will follow function) will almost immediately catch the collective eye of the purebred enthusiast and the general

A healthy litter of Tosa pups out of East West Trading
Taka, sired by Ryome.

form will be preserved by these purebred enthusiasts because they happened to like it. Louis Dobermann's Pinscher is a prime example of a breed that was bred purely for working purposes but which assumed a form that was so appealing to others that the form was preserved very quickly (as compared to other purebreds).

Other breeds remain working breeds for a long time before purebred enthusiasts take note of them. The Bulldog is a good example of a breed that went on and on, for hundreds of years, as a hard-working breed, before anyone thought to preserve its form for posterity. As a result of its having been bred purely for working purposes for so long, changes can be seen in the development of the Bulldog during its early years and dramatic changes can be observed between its general working form and the form that the show-ring ultimately decided to preserve.

(As an aside here, I must make one additional point. The Pit Bull is a rare example of a dog that ideally demonstrates form having followed function to perfection. Over the many years that the Pit Bull was bred for purely functional purposes, its form hardly changed at all. The form that early dog fighters developed was perfect for accomplishing the task at hand and as time went on, the form that had been perfected in the early days of the breed, continued to survive. It took the show-ring and the whims of novice dog owners to modify this form by selecting "bullier," larger dogs and now we have to live with the idea that The Australian Cattle Dog might be thought of as being a breed that has not been ruined by the show-ring and instead has, until now, been appreciated in its "natural" form.)

When we think of the Tosa, we should think of it more like we think of the Bulldog than as we think of such breeds as the Doberman. The Tosa has existed for over 100 years. As I have explained elsewhere, when Japanese dog fighters who were matching "lupoid" (Akita-like) dogs found themselves being beaten by the Western fighting breeds being brought to Japan by merchant seamen, they didn't stand on principal and continue to lose. They simply began crossing Western fighting breeds, the Bulldog, the Mastiff, etc., into their fighting lines and began to win again. Depending upon what was winning in the arena, "Tosa" lines might have a little of this or a little of that added to them.

This being the case, the form of the dog being produced and named after the place "Tosa" changed as time went on. Because it was only very recently that purebred enthusiasts took notice of the Tosa breed, this form has changed, on a regular basis, until recently.

Here is where some people get confused. The attitude of many elitist show-dog breeders is that if breeds are being crossed together to produce a dog that goes by the name Tosa, surely the Tosa is nothing more than a mutt, right? Wrong. With that attitude, there would be no purebred fancy at all and all of the show people would be sitting home collecting stamps. First, this is the way almost all breeds get started. But more importantly, it is an observable phenomenon that form does follow function. With all the crossbreeding that has gone on, one can still step into the middle of the world of Tosa dogs and recognize a unique form that is clearly "Tosa" and nothing else in the world of dogs. It is the job (and this, I think, is very important) of the purebred fancy, to preserve that form, whatever the breed in question may be. It is when the show-dog breeders forget to recognize the importance of function in the contribution to form, that they become the laughing stock and the butt of jokes by all serious dogmen everywhere.

Do you understand what I just tried to communicate to you? I think it is very important and so let me make sure I'm doing an adequate job of conveying what I am thinking. The specifics of the rules of the Japanese dogfight, combined with the specifics of the availability of breeds to be used by the Japanese through time, combined with the whims and fancies of the Japanese dogmen of the past and present, gave rise to a dog that is unique in the world of dogs. You can see it when you look at historical photographs of Tosa dogs of the past. One dog will look like a Bulldog, another like a St. Bernard, another like a Mastiff, and suddenly, there it is. The next photograph is the one of the Tosa. How do you know? Because as you continue to compare photographs of old and of the living dogs of today, that same, unusual, form continues to crop up, time and time again, but in only one, general place.

This is the Kochi Inu, typical of the dogs found in the Kochi area of Japan. The Kochi represents the Tosa Inu in its original form, before Western breeds were introduced into Japan. For the benefit of those who object to the Akita's being classified as a fighting dog, consider the similarity of the Kochi (a known fighting breed) and the Akita. In any event, the Tosa has always been a breed that was bred for function rather than form, and the form (from the photographs on this page and the facing page) has changed as different Western breeds were crossed into Kochi lines. These photographs illustrate the transitional forms of the Tosa.

PHOTOGRAPHS COURTESY OF DR. KATURO BABA.

Tosa form showing Great Dane influence.

Transitional Tosa form.

Tosa form showing Pointer influence.

It's hard for novice dogmen, and when I speak of "the novice" I include many prominent show-dog breeders, showmen, veterinarians, and the like, to catch the emergence of this "type." For one thing, they don't do their homework and so they don't know what they're looking at. But it is also difficult for the true dogman to keep track of this "classic type" when the demands of performance keep changing the form of so many members of the breed in question. Just when you are sure you've caught "the type" a true dogman who is interested in nothing but function, shows you what he believes is "a great Tosa," and it looks like a Pit Bull, or it looks like a Mastiff!

This leads me to the heart of the problem of today's Tosa, which is that many dogmen throughout Japan are fighting dogs in many weight categories according to different rules, depending upon how impressed the individual in question

Tosa form showing Bullmastiff
influence.

Tosa form showing Bull Terrier
influence.

Tosa form showing Bulldog
influence.

Tosa form showing the Mastiff
influence.

Old-time Tosa form.

Tosa form showing the Saint
Bernard influence.

Champion Tosa owned by Mr. Yokoshima,
wearing a ceremonial garb.

happens to be by American dogfighting rules. The two extremes in today's Tosa type are, on the one hand, the Pit Bull and on the other hand, the Mastiff. I have seen dogs that are highly regarded as Tosas that are Pit Bulls in the 70 pound range and I have seen dogs that are referred to as Tosas that are Mastiffs in the 240 plus pound range.

What does this mean? Are Tosas simply mutts? Are the breeders of these dogs liars? No. The breeders of these dogs are simply producing fighting dogs that perform best at the game they are most interested in. The guys who like the more traditional "pushing and shoving" Sumo match, prefer the Mastiff dogs. The guys who like the "game to the end," scratching contests, prefer the more Pit Bull type dogs. The important thing is that if you put all the Tosas in the world in the blender and whipped them all around for a while,

An impressive young champion Tosa
owned by Mr. Yokoshima.

what would come out is the dog that the purebred enthusiast with a trained eye would look at and immediately say "Hey, a Tosa!" Again, the distinct Tosa type emerges, time and time again, in spite of the changing fashions.

Here is something I have observed and something I wish. I have observed that the classic Tosa type is apparent only in larger dogs (120-pound males and up). I wish that classic type were available in the smaller Tosa dogs. Does this mean that something is missing among Tosas? Nope. It only means, and I will be and have been, the first to admit this, that I prefer a smaller dog. As size alone should never be the determining factor (for all the reasons I have mentioned

An athletic Tosa, Sumo from Dogstar's
kennels.

here) in establishing the quality of a Tosa, I would love to
see a good, square, well-wrinkled, classic type, fully adult
and highly capable, 80-pound male Tosa some day. Recently,
at the Tosa seminar given by Hitake Hiroshi (owner of the
Tosa-token fighting center in Kochi) in conjunction with
the annual spring rare-breed show in Washington, DC, I
asked Hiroshi if such a Tosa exists. In spite of the fact that
his English is infinitely better than my Japanese, I am not
sure that he understood the question, but the answer was
"no." My suspicion is that he understood the question and
that his answer was the definitive one. I suspect the reason
for the lack of smaller Tosas of classic type is that the Tosa

Loren Zawawi's son Jason
with his dog Toshiko.

simply is not a small dog. It is a large one, my personal preference in dogs and the preferences of some Tosa breeders not withstanding.

Anyway, you can see why so many are confused by the Tosa breed. Perhaps the future of the Tosa breed in the Western world will be even more dependent upon the solution to its other problem, which is the "fighting breed" prejudice that has risen against it. This ridiculous situation is at its most absurd in England, where I was asked to appear on live television to debate members of Parliament, representatives of the RSPCA and others, over the question of whether or not to ban the Tosa breed from the entire United Kingdom. Folks, especially in view of the fact that this legislation actually passed and stands as law, I am here to tell you that this was really something. This was truly a pathetic example of lawmakers, having been given far too much authority, and power gone awry.

To make a long story short, I made a live appearance on British TV exactly a year before I was called to speak on the Tosa issue. The first time I had been asked to debate the matter of passing an anti-Pit Bull ordinance. I went to England, I gave it my best shot, and the ordinance passed. These people were told that they couldn't own Pit Bulls and instead of "throwing the bums out," they said "Oh, OK." And that was it. Pit Bulls were totally banned.

A resting Tosa pup, bred by Steve Ostuni.

A year later, a grand total of one Tosa having found its way to the UK and this, the most docile bitch you ever imagined, similar legislation was proposed to ban Tosas. While they were at it they figured they might as well ban Fila Brasileiros and Argentine Dogos too. Although there weren't any. Some jackass had read that if there were some, they would be dangerous, so they all better be banned together. Again I was called and asked to participate in the debate. This time I

The author and his son Dan, visiting this black Tosa that was on display at a large pet expo near the author's home. Owners, Steve Ostuni and DogStar Kennels.

had to inform the television station that I was too involved in my business to leave New York just then, at which point I was asked if I would mind participating in the debate via satellite hook up! I agreed, if for no other reason that it would undoubtedly be a once in a lifetime experience.

To make another long story short, the debate was another lynch mob on another witch hunt. One silly woman declared that as the Irish Wolfhound already existed in England, there was no "need" for another large and powerful breed (watch out for the word "need" folks, and always remember that there is no "need" for anything but food, water and basic shelter). My response to this was that this being the case, all large breeds, including the Mastiff, the Newfoundland, the St. Bernard, and all others, should immediately be

Alex, the author's elder son, with a
Tosa owned by Steve Ostuni and
Serena Burnett at the pet expo.

banned from England along with the Tosa as they too were not "needed." Another described the Tosa as a "320-pound, raging, unstoppable, Pit Bull." When all was said and done, the Tosa was banned from England as the Pit Bull had been a year earlier. Both breeds are still banned today. Incidentally, the next segment of the show concerned the "need" to ban violent movies! Great place to live they've got there, eh? A real "pioneer spirit" prevails, does it not? I wonder how long it will be before we become them?

Where the Tosa has not been banned, its classification as a fighting breed has caused many to fear it, even as it has attracted many others to it. While similar classification has not done smaller, less threatening breeds, such as the

One of the author's favorite actors, the late Jack Palance, with one of his Tosas. Carl recalls Jack speaking of his Tosas on Johnny Carson's show years ago. He apparently became interested in the breed while doing an episode of *Ripley's Believe It or Not* in Japan and decided to bring home a pair.

Shar-Pei, any harm, the imposing size and the conspicuous power of the Tosa has caused many to shy away from it, if not to live in dread of it as the British apparently do.

Many of us, who take a more Libertarian approach toward life, continue to believe that the average person should continue to be allowed his basic rights (like dog ownership), and only be penalized when he or she violates the rights of others. As such, Tosa dogs continue to be available to Americans, and the popularity of this breed has been growing steadily since the publication of *The World Of Fighting Dogs*. Due to the great size of a good Tosa dog, ownership of these dogs has remained limited to those who are in a position to own very large, very powerful, dogs. I think Tosa ownership should and will remain limited to these people, and that these people should be more clear on the subject of exactly what they should be looking for in a Tosa.

Breed standards have been written according to which the Tosa has been judged at rare-breed shows throughout the United States. I wrote the first American Tosa breed standard ever to be used in judging Tosas at American rare-breed shows. I gave this standard to Don Lee of Honolulu, Hawaii (the first President of the first Tosa Association in the States) with no restrictions as to how it should be used and he distributed it freely, as I had intended it to be distributed. This standard used as its "jumping off point" a standard that had previously been published and made available to me by the JKC (Japan Kennel Club). I modified the Japanese standard only after having examined hundreds of very old and some modern photographs of Tosa dogs which were made available to me primarily by Dr. Kotoro Baba of Japan, Mr. Donald Lee of Hawaii, and others. (I have since lost contact with both Dr. Baba and Don and I wish both of them would write me so we could resume our former relationships.) Much to my amazement, I have been informed that others have taken credit for having composed this standard! This kind of thing amazes me, but is not worthy of much consideration or discussion here.

To avoid any further "confusion" about who wrote the Tosa breed standard, the standard I offer here is one that was sent to me by a representative of the Japan Kennel Club many years ago.

This impressive male goes by the name Ryomi, which means
Dragon Horse.

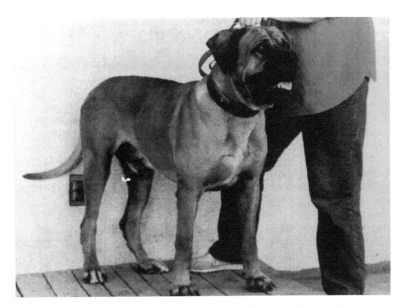

This is Keema, a male owned by Dogstar kennels.

TOSA BREED STANDARD

General Appearance: Large size dog with stately manner and robust build. The dog has hanging ears, short hair, square muzzle, dewlap, and hanging tail, thick root. The temperament is noteworthy for patience, composure, boldness, and courageousness.

Size: Minimum height 60½ centimeters for dogs, 54½ centimeters for bitches.

Head: The skull, broad; stop rather abrupt; the muzzle, moderately long. The nasal bridge, straight; the nose, large and black. The upper and lower jaws, strong; and teeth, strong with strong canine teeth and scissors bite.

Eyes: Relatively small and dark brown in color with expression of dignity.

Ears: Relatively small, rather thin, and set on high of skull sides, hanging close to cheeks.

Neck: Muscular with dewlap.

Body: The withers, high, back, level, and straight. The loins, broad and muscular; croup, slightly arched at top. The chest, broad and deep; ribs, moderately sprung. The belly well drawn up.

Tail: Set on high, thick at root, and tapering to the end, which reaches the hocks.

Forequarters and Hindquarters: The shoulders, moderately sloping. The forearms, straight, moderately long, and strong. The pasterns, slightly inclining and robust. Muscles of hind legs, very developed. The joints of stifle and hock, moderately angled and vigorous.

Feet: Tightly closed. The pads, thick and elastic. The nails, hard and dark in color (desirable).

Gait: Robust and powerful.

Coat: Short, hard, and dense.

Color: Solid red is ideal, but white and red markings also permitted.

Disqualifications: Monorchid or cryptorchid.

Major Faults: Shyness. Thin bone. Extremely overshot or undershot.

Minor Faults: Snipey muzzle. Slightly overshot or undershot.

Ready for business, folks, and still smiling: a champion Tosa in ceremonial fighting dress in the arena.

As I said earlier, I now have my doubts that the ideal Tosa will ever be found among smaller (80-pound) dogs. The classic type is steeped in the genealogy of various Mastiff breeds and as these are very large dogs, so will the Tosa very

A good-looking black Tosa bitch
owned by Mr. Sisaki of Japan.

likely remain large. Nevertheless, I would love to see an 80-pound, typologically correct male Tosa. It is a dog the world of purebred ownership will respond to in a big way, I can assure you. The race for the largest dog goes on among Tosa owners, as it does among owners of so many other breeds, but it is a meaningless and anti-productive goal. Tosa breeders should be worrying more about preserving type than gaining size. A sturdy, athletic, large-headed, well-wrinkled, Tosa is fine at 120 pounds and would be of great interest at 80 pounds. At 155 pounds, one is dealing with a very large dog that will hold limited appeal for American dog fanciers, but which is very historically correct. Size beyond a trim 155 pounds, plus or minus a few pounds, is unnecessary for Tosa males, in my opinion.

When all is said and done, living with a Tosa is for a select group of dog owners regardless of the size of the dog in question. For the first time owner, the Tosa is a poor choice. For the smaller home or apartment owner, the Tosa is again a poor choice. The Tosa is a large dog that needs "enough" space. It is a low-keyed dog and so may require less room than some may think it would, but any dog needs the room to wag its tail without fear of breaking something.

The Tosa should be by nature, dog aggressive. After all, the Tosa is undeniably a fighting dog and a Tosa that is not dog aggressive would be less than what the breed was intended to be, wouldn't it? (Remember, even the AKC show standard for the Akita calls for a dog that is aggressive toward other dogs). A dog-aggressive dog requires a responsible owner. This is not to say that a Tosa cannot be protective when raised at home, but it is to say that if you are looking for a readily, outwardly man-aggressive dog, you would do well to look among other guardian breeds before looking to the Tosa. I have had serious Tosa breed enthusiasts from the early days of the breed describe the Tosa as being downright dangerous to own when it is outwardly man demands a large and powerful owner if it is to be walked among other dogs. Walking a dog-aggressive, 100-pound plus dog is no job for a young person or for a smaller person regardless of age.

Toward man, the Tosa should not be unnecessarily aggressive. Not only is there no need for a very man-aggressive dog among fighting dogs, but the specifics of the Japanese dogfight demand that a handler should be able to pull these dogs apart while fighting without fear aggressive, and utterly useless as a home guardian when it is not.

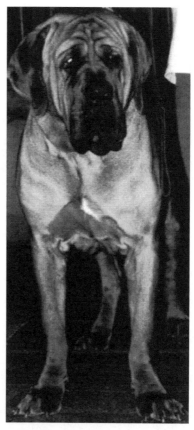

Top left: Cherry, an athletic Dogstar Tosa bitch. *Middle left:* Young East West Tosa bitch with Steve Ostuni and Mr. Sisaki. *Bottom left:* Steve Ostuni with a champion Tosa owned by the Hirose family. The author met the younger Hirose at the American Rare Breed Association's Cherry blossom show some years ago. *Above:* Ryoma, co-owned by Dogstar and East West, is from the Hirose Fighting Center in Kochi, Japan.

145

A Tosa match taking place in Japan.

Fortunately, few Tosas were outwardly man aggressive in the early days of the breed in the United States, and I have not heard of any highly man-aggressive Tosas either in Japan or on the American mainland in a long time.

As a pet the Tosa can be a fine dog, in the right home. One day, I had a couple of dog enthusiast friends over for a barbecue. One was Chief Geriy Pleasant of the Hartford, Connecticut Police Department. The other was the rare-breed judge, Todd Fenstermacher. I hadn't told either Todd or Gerry (or their wives, Lydia and Maria) that Steve Ostuni of East/West Kennels in Georgia and Serina Burnett of Dog Star Kennels in California were due to come over with a beautiful, calm, Tosa bitch they co-owned. Steve and Serina let me walk the bitch into the house, to Todd and Gerry's delight. In no time flat, the 160-pound bitch had curled up on the rug in our den, at everyone's feet, and was content to watch everyone chat as the kids played with its tail and its ears. When Steve and Serina left, the conversation was about

146

almost nothing but how all of us would love to own a Tosa like the one that had just visited us. It was a fine looking animal and a calm steady dog as well, but large none the less. The Tosa should only be considered for ownership by those who can deal with its size for the duration of the animal's life.

A very fine pair of Tosas owned by Steve Ostuni.

Akihito of Tamahimeden, owned and
bred by K. Jessen of Heinsberg,
Germany, represents the muscular
conformation and head that breeders
are striving for today.

East West Trading California Dog.

Above and below: Championship ceremonial garb, collar and robe. Courtesy of Dogstar kennels and Mr. Sisaki.

Above left: Champion Tosa owned by Mr. Yokoshima of Japan in ceremonial fighting costume. *Above right:* Male Tosa owned by the Hiroses with Steve Ostuni, photographed in gift shop at the Tosa Fighting Center. *Below*: The Tosa Fighting Center in Kochi, Japan.

A BRIEF
INTRODUCTION TO
BULL TERRIER BREEDS

Although I will go on to discuss the American Pit Bull Terrier, the American Staffordshire Terrier, Staffordshire Bull Terrier, and the Bull Terrier in separate chapters, I would like to take this time to discuss them together because there has been so much misunderstanding surrounding these dogs. A great deal of this misunderstanding stems from ignorance, but some stems from a well grounded difference of opinion. Examples of the two extremes are as follows:

Only last evening I walked into a local video store to rent a movie for my family and I to watch. The guy behind the counter noticed that I was wearing a T-shirt advertising "Rode Hawg." American Bulldog kennels. The shirt had been given to me by Lariy Koura, who operates Rode Hawg. When the counter guy in the video store noticed the T-shirt he began to explain to me that American Bulldogs were not the same as Pit Bulls. He explained that there were three distinct breeds that the average dog enthusiast often confused, these being the Pit Bull, the American Bull and the American Staffordshire Terrier.

I informed the counter fellow that I was aware of the difference between a Pit Bull and an American Bull and the more I spoke, the more likely he became to ask questions rather than to answer them. Finally, he decided to ask my advice about an upcoming breeding he had planned. The breeding was a brother to sister breeding, the dogs in question being litter-mates. He wanted to know if I thought it was a good idea. I told him that only under rare circumstances could such a close in-breeding be justified and I asked him if he had a very good reason for considering this breeding. He assured me that he had a very good reason. I asked him what the reason was. He informed me that the reason was that both the dog and the bitch had papers. That was the reason. Needless to say, I advised him against breeding dogs altogether.

But on the other end of the spectrum are those who know the Pit Bull breed well, who have thought through the question of whether the Pit Bull and the American Staffordshire Terrier (in particular) are one breed or two, and who have arrived at the conclusion that they are separate breeds. The thinking is that as the American Staffordshire Terrier has been bred for nothing but show purposes for so

This smiling American Pit Bull Terrier is Champion Blinky from Germany. The author thanks photographer Markus Rogen for the ton of great pictures of Pit Bulls and other breeds from Germany. These professional shots capture terrific-looking dogs at work and play and really have made this book look sensational!

long, while the Pit Bull has, over the years, been largely "game bred," these dogs now look so different from each other, think so different from each other, and operate on such different levels of physical ability, that the two breeds can no longer be thought of as being the same.

This line of thinking is not as utterly ignorant of breed history as it may at first seem to be to some Pit Bull and Am Staff enthusiasts. In defense of this position, that I myself do not support, let me play devil's advocate and point out that it is far from unheard of in the world of purebred dogs for two breeds which are accepted as being entirely distinct to have identical genetic backgrounds. In trying to keep this

It can be argued that the American Staffordshire Terrier is an entirely different breed from the American Pit Bull Terrier, as Am Staff breeders have concentrated solely on conformation and not ability.

argument as close to the original as possible, let me ask you to consider the American Pit Bull Terrier (UKC/ADBA etc.) and the little AKC variety Boston Terrier for a moment. Are these breeds the same?

Most, if not all, purebred enthusiasts would maintain the position that the Pit Bull and the Boston are entirely different dogs. Indeed, the two breeds look completely different. They are of very different size. But how many purebred enthusiasts who consider these dogs to be different breeds are aware of

Natural smilers, American Pit Bull Terriers are good lookers and good fighters.

the history of each breed and of the genetic background of each of these breeds?

One of the great dog books, written in 1921 by Dr. William A. Bruette, includes a chapter on the Boston Terrier. (As an aside, I own a first edition copy of this book along with a two-part series of books entitled *Forest and Stream Sportsmen's Encyclopedia,* copyright 1923, also by Bruette.) The *Forest and Stream* books are purely hunting, fishing, wild animals, and hunting dogs. I'll be quoting from the original *Complete Dog Book,* but I believe this book has been reissued by my original publisher, T.F.H. If you haven't got it, you might want to pick it up. It's good reading. Furthermore, the old books give us great insight into where today's dogs came from and so, what they should be today.

By the way, Bruette's *The Complete Dog Book* contains virtually no pictures. These were the days when it was

Pit Bulls, as a breed, more so than German Shepherds or Dobermans, are bred for performance and as such make suitable choices for protection work. The author contends that a higher percentage of Pit Bulls is bred for performance than most of the so-called protection breeds.

information that people "read" dog books for. Imagine trying to get a dog book published without pictures today! But of the very few pictures he does include, two are of a game-looking little Boston, and another two are of a very fine looking, white Bull Terrier. (What a guy, this Bruette was, eh?)

In the Boston Terrier chapter of Bruette's book, he says of the Boston that "... all that can be learned of their ancestry points to their having been of Pit Bull origin." Other sources, both old and modern, agree that either the Boston was directly bred from Pit Bull lines or the breed was produced using the same parent breeds, the Bulldog of old, the now extinct, English White Terrier, and possibly other Terriers that were used in the production of the Pit Bull. So why

These two smiling white Bull Terriers are Gorgona Taiss and Arledino Archie Caprisse from Russia.

don't Pit Bulls and Bostons look the same? Going back to Bruette we read that "... Pit Bulls are usually the result of a cross between bulldogs and terriers, and vary in form. Some have the long, clean head of a terrier; others, the round, almost puggish head of the bulldog. The rounded-headed, short-faced brindle dogs that were a result of these crosses could not win against the terrier types in their own classes, and as they were crowded out their admirers succeeded in having classes organized for them, and these classes were eventually recognized by the AKC."

Isn't that interesting, for a number of reasons? Hopefully the ears of modern Pit Bull, American Staffordshire Terrier, and Staffordshire Bull Terrier breeders, judges, enthusiasts, etc., perked up when they read that the bull-type dogs were not sufficiently competitive with the terrier-type dogs. For the most part, the bulldogs may look good, but winning the dogfight isn't about looks, is it? Furthermore, creating a "show dog" that is not representative of its working counterpart is not what the show is all about either, is it?

So, as Bruette has pointed out, it was merely selective breeding from within the same gene pool that gave rise to the distinction between the Boston Terrier and the Pit Bull. As such, it is not so far-fetched for some to maintain that selective breeding for looks, on the part of AKC show people, and game breeding by Pit Bull enthusiasts, has brought about the emergence of a new breed, entirely distinct from the Pit Bull, in the American Staffordshire Terrier. After all, you can tell a game-bred Pit Bull from an Am Staff when you look at it. The dogfighting underground has long since proven that the show variety Am Staff can't stay with a game bred Pit Bull in the pits, so they are different dogs, as are the Boston Terrier and the Pit Bull.

Having said this all, I totally disagree with the above. In my opinion, not only are the Pit Bull and the Am Staff the same breed, but so is the Staffordshire Bull Terrier simply another expression of the same breed too. The Bull Terrier is another breed. In the production of the Bull Terrier, James Hinks bred back to the Terrier at least once because he, like Bruette, also observed that the more Terrier type dogs did all the consistent winning. What Hinks ultimately proved, in spite of himself, was that some terrier is a good thing, but too much terrier does not produce a winning dog.

Why is it so difficult for some Pit Bull enthusiasts to fathom that the Pit Bull, the Am Staff and, to a lesser extent, the Staff Bull are all the same breed? After all, are show Airedales and working Airedales the same? Do they look the same? Are they equally capable in the field? They are not. Are working Chesapeake Bay Retrievers (another favorite breed of mine) and show Chesapeakes the same? Do they look the same to the trained eye? They sure don't act the same. In many breeds we can clearly observe a "working" variety and a "show" variety within the breed and we all understand why the two don't look the same. Why should the Pit Bull be any different? Why can't we understand that the old style Pit Bull is simply the working expression of the same breed that the American Staffordshire Terrier belongs to?

I think there are a number of answers to this question. For one thing, there's the name difference to contend with. The American Pit Bull Terrier and the American Staffordshire Terrier are registered under different breed names. This difference in breed names, however, was never intended to convey that the Am Staff is not the same breed as the Pit Bull. The AKC, upon registering the Pit Bull back in the 1930s, simply decided to stay clear of the name Pit Bull because of the pit fighting connotation. They used the name Staffordshire Terrier (later, American Staffordshire Terrier) to convey that their dogs were an American expression of the fighting bull and terrier dogs of Staffordshire, England. And what were these fighting bull and terrier dogs of Staffordshire? They were Staffordshire Bull Terrier dogs, of course!

Shakespeare reminds us that 'That which we call a rose, by any other name would smell as sweet." This being the case with dogs, as with roses, the real reason that the Pit Bull fraternity is, by and large, unwilling to accept the fact that the Pit Bull and the Am Staff are the same dog goes beyond breed names. It has been my observation that "the real reason" the Pit Bull fraternity (what's left of it) refuses to accept the Am Staff as being the same breed as the Pit Bull has more to do with its distaste for the people behind the Am Staff than it does its distaste for the Am Staff itself.

Pit Bull enthusiasts have long been frustrated by their breed having been assigned the status of second-class citizen as compared to the Am Staff. Although many are either unwilling or unable to clearly verbalize the cause of their frustration, what this cause is, is the realization that the show dog fancy turns up its nose at the Pit Bull. The game-bred Pit Bull is rarely as impressive looking a dog, to the novice's eye, as the show-ring Pit Bull is. A game-bred dog will often have more leg under it. Its head will often not be as broad. Its chest will often not be as wide. Its body will often not be as square, and the dog will often not be as large. But it is the game-bred form that is the prototype of the breed. It is the game-bred form that the show, in its naivete, is trying to duplicate and preserve. The show dog differs from the game dog in appearance not because of the game dogmen's naivete, but because of the show dogmen's lack of familiarity with the subject of dogs.

This is why the game dogman becomes frustrated. This frustration often expresses itself in the form of utter distaste and this distaste aims itself at the Am Staff. Frankly, over the years, I have noticed that this desire for a "bullier" outward appearance has even taken its toll on the game-bred dog. Many game dogmen may continue to breed what wins, but what wins is what comes out of a yard of a man who sometimes has a preference for a bullier dog. We'll talk more about this later.

Furthermore, as time goes on, game-bred stock accounts for a smaller and smaller percentage of dogs from within the

Friar Tuck's Highspeed, a Bull Terrier bred by
Rudolf Sewerin of Germany, is a fine protection
dog. Sewerin selects for working qualities in
his BTs, unlike some American breeders. The
author sees far too many scatterbrained dogs
in the US for the breed to be of serious interest
to him.

breed we know as the American Pit Bull Terrier. The United Kennel Club (UKC), once a game-dog registry organization, has long since become heavily involved in the show, and their dogs reflect this. Even the American Dog Breeder's Association (ADBA) is currently registering some American Pit Bull Terriers that are very unlike the smaller, terrier type, Pit Bulls of game-bred stock. In fact, as I am sitting here writing this, I have open before me a copy of the ADBA quarterly publication, *American Pit Bull Terrier Gazette,* and there is a picture looking back at me of an 11-month-old "Pit Bull" pup that is 107 pounds.

I ask you this. If the claim of some dogmen is that we can no longer consider the American Staffordshire Terrier and the American Pit Bull Terrier to be the same breed because the American Staffordshire Terrier has been produced for purely show purposes for so long at this point that it no longer has either the appearance or the physical ability of the game-bred Pit Bull, then how many breeds is the "American Pit Bull Terrier?"

In other words, if the Am Staff and the game-bred Pit Bull are so different now that they constitute separate breeds, aren't the game-bred Pit Bull and the show variety, purebred, UKC Pit Bull also separate breeds? And aren't the game-bred Pit Bull and the 107-pound, 11-month-old, Pit Bull also separate breeds? Do you see what I am saying here? If we are going to ignore the fact that these dogs all represent different expressions of the same breed, and begin to split hairs instead, then we have more hairs to split than just the two which are most often split.

But where does the Staffordshire Bull fit into all of this? If the Pit Bull and the Am Staff are the same breed, and

Two intimidating Am Staffs named Evil and Baby,
owned by Tough Guy kennels in Austria.

if the Pit Bull is essentially the American expression of
the Staffordshire Bull, why is it that the Am Staff and the
Staff Bull are not only so different today, but constitute two
distinct breeds in the eyes of the AKC and others? This gets
complicated and I will ask the reader to study the chapters on
these "three breeds" in order to gain a fuller understanding of
what is going on here. In the meantime, the following must
suffice.

It makes some sense to me that the Pit Bull and the Staff
Bull don't look exactly the same. After all, although these
dogs may have all been the same once (the Staff Bull having
been the fighting dog of the coal miners of Staffordshire,
England), upon having been brought to the United States,
3,000 miles away and an ocean apart as well, these dogs began
to change in form. Why wouldn't they? People of similar
mind, but different people with a different set of preferences

Baron is a friendly American-bred Staffordshire Bull Terrier who competes successfully in dog shows.

never the less, undertook the breeding of these dogs in the United States. As with so many other things done by we Americans, we decided the Staff Bull needed more size. We modified the Staff Bull to make it the model of fighting dogs. We made it bigger, as a breed.

Also, in the States, the "heat was largely off" the dogfighting fraternity. England was a comparatively small place with a zillion regulations. We offered dog fighters and the sport of dogfighting a huge place with relatively few regulations. Dog fighters could go on to perfect the gamest of fighting dogs in the States, while in the mother country of the fighting dogs, less and less was being done to put the breed forward at its game and fewer were willing to become involved.

The upshot of this was that the Staff Bull and the Pit Bull began to look different from each other. The dog the Am Staff enthusiast originally intended to "preserve" then was

164

Mickey, a Pit Bull bred by Rudolf Schwab of France, imported to the US and registered as an American Staffordshire Terrier. Mickey is a great protection dog and the sire of many other capable Pit Bulls today.

not the Staff Bull but the Pit Bull, as it had been developed in the States. As the showman's imagination began to introduce its own, atypical ideas into the blueprint of the Am Staff, this "three in one" breed began to evolve even more. The Am Staff became not the showman's expression of the Staff Bull, but rather the showman's expression of that expression of the Pit Bull which evolved in the dog pits of the United States, "i.e.," the American Pit Bull Terrier.

I think we're getting more involved here than I want to be in this chapter. I would prefer that you read and understand the breed chapters devoted to each of these breeds than that you delve any further into this problem now. Suffice, at this point, to say that as far as I am concerned, I see more of the game, but fun loving Pit Bull of old preserved in the form of the Staffordshire Bull Terrier (as it is being produced in England today) then I do in the American Staffordshire Terrier. But this is not to say that the show world, and the world of backyard, big, bully dog breeders, hasn't impacted the look and the mind of the Pit Bull breed as well.

AMERICAN PIT BULL TERRIER

I think that as we head into this chapter on the American Pit Bull Terrier, it is important that we take a minute to remind ourselves of the goal of this book. The primary goal of this book is not to discuss the breeds I talk about in it from the ground up. I've already done this in my previously published and currently available books. The goal of this book is to discuss the changes that have taken place as regards each of these breeds and this entire subject generally.

Having watched the popularity of the Pit Bull (American Pit Bull Terrier) breed explode over the course of the last couple decades, I have made a mental note, and now a literary note, of changes that have affected the shape (physical shape, mental condition, etc.) of this, and other breeds discussed

A black-nose red dog with his trophy in Germany.

here, as their popularity exploded. From my perspective, the Pit Bull was just perfect as it was when I found it, and as any alteration of perfection can only mean that a state of something less than perfection has been created, I am not happy with any of these changes. Before discussing the changes in the Pit Bull breed, let's talk about what it is that was, and still is responsible for these changes.

Through the 1970s the condition of the Pit Bull breed was quite different than it is today. Until about 1980 or so, the Pit Bull was of limited interest to purebred enthusiasts. Dog lovers, who simply wanted to own a good dog, occasionally found the Pit Bull breed and adopted it, but these discoveries were few and far between. For the most part, these dogs were owned by people (primarily Americans but some "Native Americans," some Canadians and some Mexicans (matches were staged on reservation land, in Canada, and in Mexico,

B&Ws Champion Spice was one of the gamest stud dogs in
Germany and among the most famous Pit Bulls in Europe.

as well as in parts of the United States, primarily the South)
who were interested in dogfighting. As an aside, from among
fighting dog litters, some pups found their way to "family"
homes and passed their lives as great family dogs. Those who
owned these dogs were either dog fighters or owners who
were interested in keeping a dog like this back in the days
when there was no public stigma against them. Also, the
flip side of there being no public stigma against the breed
was that it held no appeal to the "just get me a macho dog"
crowd. When I got my first Pit Bull, back in 1971, those
who saw my dog on the street would literally cross the street
to set their children upon it so that the kids could play with
the "Petey" dog. So what went wrong? How did this breed's
reputation change so much?

Champion Hope is a German pit dog.

At Some point during the early 1980s, the public discovered the Pit Bull. Dick Stratton's first book was published in 1977. Stratton had already written about the Pit Bull for well-circulated dog magazines, but these magazines were read primarily by those who were already interested in a select group of purebreds. Stratton's first book extolled the virtues of the Pit Bull. Did he interest an abundance of novices in this breed? Was the stage already set for an explosion in the popularity of the Pit Bull and did Stratton's book merely anticipate and respond to this brewing interest? Can we "blame" Stratton for "Pit Bullmania?"

In my first book, I introduced many breeds which were virtually unknown to the American dog fancy, among them the American Bulldog, the Tosatoken, and the Bordeaux Dogue. Especially in the case of the American Bulldog, the stage is set for all hell to break loose as amateurs to dog ownership find themselves way over their heads in American Bulldog ownership. To a minor extent, trouble has already risen among those who were unable to control their American Bulldogs, but the general public's lack of familiarity with the American Bulldog breed spared it close scrutiny. Incidents in which Bulldogs were involved were written off to the Pit Bull problem, and the Pit Bull breed took the heat. I have been asked if I feel guilty of having introduced this, and other breeds, to novice dog owners. I have been asked if I feel guilty of having fanned the flames of "Pit Bullmania" by telling all the world, in no uncertain terms, that of all breeds, the Pit Bull is my favorite. My answer is an unequivocal "Don't be absurd," and I'll tell you why.

Dick Stratton wrote a book. I wrote a book. Sam Colt patented a gun. In each case, each man announced to the world what interested him. Sam Colt patented a revolver that he used responsibly. He did it for the good of mankind. When he made it available to the world, there is no doubt in my mind that he did so in order to provide good men with a good gun. In my opinion, it is high time that we, as a people, begin to see the difference between those who use things responsibly and those who do not. Where would the world be if the person who invented the wheel, thought the matter through to its end, realized that if he gave this idea to the world, someone would eventually be hit by a car, and squashed the idea in order to save the lives that would be lost?

Richard Stratton knows the Pit Bull breed well. He enjoys owning Pit Bulls and, to the best of my knowledge, he owns them responsibly. He saw that the dog fancy generally was unaware of the breed, and he did mankind the favor of bringing the good news to others. It was not Stratton's responsibility to anticipate the abuse of the breed and to withhold information in the fear that the information he provided would be misused. It was mankind's responsibility to use the information that Stratton provided responsibly, and it should remain the responsibility of those who earn their livings insuring both the public safety and the public's liberty to deal with those who misuse those items which, in the hands of a responsible person, would be nothing but a safe and fun to shoot sporting rifle, a safe and fun to be with, family dog, etc.

Are Pit Bulls good guard dogs? Dr. Semencic's challenge: "I'd like to ask anyone who maintains that a Pit Bull is not a good guard dog if he'd be willing to break into a house with this dog in it while I ran some video footage of the event."

We are unfortunately two decades into the explosion in popularity of the Pit Bull breed, and it has long since

ZWs Dana from Germany.

become obvious to all, that many people throughout the world are unable to breed, sell and own even a simple dog properly. Numerous tragedies have occurred involving Pit Bulls. In some instances dogs were poorly raised and, being misunderstood by their owners, were left in situations in which sometimes a child, sometimes an adult, was hurt by the dog in question. In other instances, Pit Bulls were actually used as weapons by unscrupulous owners who intentionally set them upon people. This very day, the newspapers are abuzz with a story of two Pit Bulls who were left alone with their owner's parents for a long weekend. The bottom line of this story is that one parent was actually killed by one of the Pit Bulls and the other parent was badly "mauled." These situations are almost unimaginably horrible for anyone to hear about, let alone for someone to experience.

The general public has about had it with such horror stories and while some areas have already passed legislation banning Pit Bull ownership, many other areas are seriously considering such legislation. Pit Bull advocates point out that the Pit Bull is actually less likely to bite than many other breeds are, only to be faced with the argument that while a Cocker Spaniel may be much more likely to bite a person than a Pit Bull is, it is completely unlikely to savage a human being to the extent that a Pit Bull can. These people do not take the time to consider what a great many breeds are currently available to potential dog owners (and have long been available to potential dog owners) that could also savage a person beyond the possibility of self defense and how, as a result, it doesn't make sense to single out the Pit Bull from among these many breeds, but the collective mind of the other side has already been closed in the wake of all the horror stories brought to us by the mass media.

This German Pit Bull is chewing on a pig's ear. In Europe, the dogs are still intended for use as catch dogs during their adulthood. This gives pups a taste for their future job.

Personally, I am old enough to remember when the kind of reputation that precedes the Pit Bull breed today was assigned to other breeds. The Doberman Pinscher, when I was a child, had precisely the same reputation that the Pit Bull has today. For quite a while, the St. Bernard, of all the innocuous breeds, also had this same cross to bear. Today the Doberman is presented by the media as being little more than Pit Bull food, while no one in his right mind panics at the sight of a St. Bernard, the movie *Cujo* not withstanding. Meanwhile, when I was a child and when I was a young man, and before my time, absolutely no one feared the Pit Bull! The breed carried with it nothing more than the Petey of the "Our Gang" comedy series reputation, and that's it. I clearly remember people snickering at my little dog and wondering why anyone would want such a funny-looking little animal.

So when will this public fear of the Pit Bull blow over, if ever, how will it blow over, and what will be responsible for its blowing over? It has been my observation that the stage is already set for "Pit Bullmania" to pass us by. Already the general public is shifting its collective interest to larger, more impressive-looking dogs that will also respond to an owners direction to conduct themselves in an unruly manner. I get call after call about serious problems that people, nationwide, are having with their Akita dogs. The Rottweiler has become among the most popular breeds to be registered with the American Kennel Club, and the reports have already begun to come across the airwaves of serious, sometimes deadly, Rottweiler attacks upon human beings.

The Pit Bull will be replaced by other potentially dangerous (in the wrong hands) breeds of dogs. Hopefully there will be a day (and hopefully I will live to see it) when

Jazzman with Grand Champion Smith.

a select few will care to own Pit Bulls and when the general public will scratch its head and say to itself, "Remember when it was the Pit Bull breed we all thought was so dangerous? What ever happened to those dogs anyway?" I worry sometimes that as the AKC, in the maintenance of its position that breed-specific legislation is absurd, will begin to look more and more like the poor NRA to some people, and that when, and if, breed-specific legislation is passed, it will come down upon us as it has been proposed by many would be lawmakers in this country. It could take a more sweeping form than many of us expect and many breeds will be banned together. Who knows? If we can throw out the Bill of Rights and ban guns, it should be easy for lawmakers to ban dogs, shouldn't it?

A highly game Pit Bull running the
wheel, which is a big, carpeted wooden
circle on a spindle. The dog is chained
to the post and was running for no
apparent reason other than it felt like it.

In addition to a dramatic change in the public perception
of the American Pit Bull Terrier breed (and along with it, all
related bull and terrier breeds) since the publication of my
first book, my own perception of the breed has changed as
well. It has been my observation that this breed has changed
in both form and in function. It has changed in form because
the novices who got involved in it from 1977 until the present
period were unhappy with the breed's typically unimpressive,

Gerry Pleasant with his dual-registered
American Pit Bull Terrier/American
Staffordshire Terrier. This dog is
overdone for the author's taste, but
Gerry likes this big, blocky look.

terrier-like appearance. It changed in function because this
same new crop of novice owners were generally completely
uninterested in the definitive quality of this breed (the very
essence of the breed), its "gameness." What they wanted
was a hard-hitting dog that would be impressive in a short
fight. They wanted a man-stopping dog and they wanted a
dog that could dispatch the next-door neighbor's German
Shepherd in 30 seconds. The concept of owning a dog of

world championship caliber was, and is, utterly foreign to them. Instead, they wanted most the very kind of dog that serious dogmen want least, that kind of Pit Bull commonly referred to by dogmen as "a front running cur."

Regarding the form of the breed, it is an embarrassingly American phenomenon that everything bigger is regarded as being better. Many American dog breeders in search of a tough dog are not satisfied with the dog that has been proven to be the single toughest dog in the world! In his breeding program he will often not try to duplicate this dog. Instead, he will try to recreate it, only bigger, the concept being that if a 50-pound dog can be really tough, a 100-pound dog will be twice as tough. I don't know why so many of us think this way. Is it the fact that we have so much more space to own large things than our European and Asian brethren have?

The first thing many American purebred enthusiasts will tell you about their dogs is how big they are. "My German Shepherd weighs 135 pounds!" Never mind the fact that it is completely lame and it looks great only when lying on a scale. "My Pit Bull weighs 90 pounds!" Never mind that it can't get out of its own way as compared to a better Pit Bull of half its size. As this mentality got its paws on the Pit Bull breed, the breed immediately jumped in size. Most of these owners, and many of these breeders, have no idea what size a proper Pit Bull should be; they simply prefer a dog that is large. A few have actually studied some Pit Bull breed history and use as their defense of their preference for larger dogs the fact that the occasional large dog did crop up in the yards of some of the well-known old-time dogmen. (Colby's Pincher from the earliest part of the 20th century, etc.) They ignore the fact that the larger dogs were the exception to the

ZWs Ali running the treadmill in Germany.

rule and that to breed dogs that are bigger than the biggest of the old-time dogs is to change the form of the Pit Bull breed overall. Today's "novice stock" Pit Bull is generally larger than the Pit Bull of yesteryear, and to make any changes in that which is perfect is to create something that is less than perfect, in my opinion.

Today's "novice stock" (as opposed to today's fine game-bred stock) Pit Bull is also "bullier" than the Pit Bulls of the earlier days of this fine breed. Years ago, the guys who counted among their passions in life their participation in the sport of matching game dogs liked a dog that could win in a dog match according to the rules. They didn't care if their dog was broad skulled and broad chested as long as it won and made its owner proud. Occasionally a relatively bully-looking dog cropped up from among fighting-dog litters that did well in sport, but this dog would be bred to a winning bitch and a winning bitch only, regardless of the looks of the bitch, or the potential looks of the puppies the mating in question would produce. A winning dog, or a dog from winning lines, looked good to its owner and that was that. (Bear in mind, these great dogs of old still exist today in the yards of game dogmen, but they are not what the average novice "gimme a mean dog" owner keeps. Unfortunately, these novice owners have become the majority of Pit Bull owners today.)

Champion Fox, now deceased, was a littermate to Grand Champion Badger, considered to be one of the finest 34-pound dogs ever bred.

A German red-nosed red Pit Bull. The author has featured many dogs from around the world in this book to demonstrate that the Pit Bull and other breeds do not have a one-country following. Should one country outlaw one or all of these breeds, it is likely that these breeds will still thrive elsewhere. Pit Bull folk, regardless of where they live, are important to the preservation of the breed.

Whereas once a large percentage of Pit Bull owners actually matched, or at least game tested their dogs, today a very small minority of Pit Bull owners and breeders actually requires that their breed be able to perform well at the task for which these dogs were intended. Many don't care about a Pit Bull's ability to fight another dog at all. What they are interested in is a dog's outward appearance only. These are primarily the show people, who often pride themselves upon their breeding of dogs with no brains and no character. They want a good-looking dog that they can sell with confidence that it will never hurt a fly. Paradoxically, far more man-biting Pit Bulls have come from lines like these than from game-bred lines.

Childhood friend of Dr. Semencic, this is Greg Jackson with Conan, now deceased. This Pit Bull the author found to be entirely too intense. It was good looking and would kill anyone who touched his owner, overly aggressive toward man and beast, an undesirable trait in any dog.

Others want an exceptionally tough-looking dog for guardian purposes. These tough-looking dogs should not only be big and powerful looking, unlike many of the greatest fighting dogs of all time, but should also be willing to demonstrate a man-aggressive and often dog-aggressive nature. In my opinion, this is where the bulk of today's truly dangerous Pit Bulls are coming from. Breeders of dogs like these sell their pups for big money to breeders of some of the gamest pit dogs in the country.

(As an aside, it is important to remember here that game dogmen of the past and present have absolutely no use for a Pit Bull that has any desire to bite a man. This very afternoon I spoke with three novices who insist upon forcing the Pit Bull to be something that it is not by nature: a man-aggressive, outwardly aggressive dog. The fact that these big, tough-looking Pit Bulls are selectively bred to be dangerous, combined with the fact that they are generally raised by poor owners who teach them to be dangerous, creates a dangerous dog that ends up giving this entire breed a bad reputation. The first assured me that he didn't have a dog in his yard that would bite a man, and in fact, my younger son Dan and I were perfectly comfortable walking right into the litterbox of good bitches that were nursing pups. This precipitated nothing more than a wag of the tail on the part of the bitch. The second game dogman told me he didn't know what a man-biting Pit Bull was, as he had never owned one. Meanwhile, he had 66 pit dogs in his yard as we spoke. The third, a very famous game dogman, referred to man-biting Pit Bulls as "an aberration." What does this tell us but that the willing man-biter among pit dogs is really just a concoction created by novice Pit Bull owners, and that these dogs certainly do not define this breed in its pure form.)

Think about the desirability of a man-biting Pit Bull, Tosa, American Bulldog, etc., for a minute. In each case, the dogs mentioned, when being used for work in the area for which it was developed, must be handled by a man, often a strange man, while it is demonstrating its peak of aggressive behavior. The Pit Bull, working in the dog pit, must be

A determined-looking pit dog from Germany. The author has found that a collar provides greater control over a dog than a harness. A collar gives the handler control of the dog's head, and that's the part that can be a liability.

A German Pit Bull with his new trophy. There is no better all-purpose home guardian and general "buddy" than a Pit Bull, but an owner must approach keeping a dog like this with complete responsibility. It's a shame that so much irresponsible ownership has given this great breed such a bad reputation.

handled by a handler who has no desire to be attacked by either the dog he is handling, or that dog's opponent. The Tosa is also handled while in the fighting arena. The American Bulldog is sometimes fought against other dogs, so requiring that it is handled while it is being matched. Other American Bulldogs are used for catching wild range hogs. Under these conditions, the dog is completely focused upon its intended prey, but it must never consider attacking either the man who will come to finish the hog, or any of the hounds that have brought this hog to bay. In none of these situations could a man-biting dog be tolerated.

Still others among Pit Bull people, and this segment of the Pit Bull-owning and breeding population is getting bigger and bigger all the time, want Pit Bulls that not only look impressive but which can actually be impressive in a short dogfight. Only the day before yesterday, I got a call from a reporter for a major newspaper in Connecticut. The purpose of her call was to collect information for an article she was doing that would be written in response to the explosion in popularity of "on the street" Pit Bull fighting!

This is not a "sport" that is unique to Connecticut alone. I have heard numerous reports of this going on in New York City, in areas of New Jersey, and elsewhere . Apparently, what many backyard breeders and pit fighters are doing is getting together on street corners, in public parks, out in the open, and matching dogs in prearranged, fairly big money matches. Unlike the serious dog match, for obvious reasons, these matches are rarely allowed to go on for any great length of time. A winner is declared on the basis of its having damaged its opponent quickly, and not on the strength of its gameness. Dogs that are bred to do well in this kind of contest are not

There's many a good-looking Pit Bull living in Europe today and around the world.

necessarily the same kind of dogs that do well in the old-fashioned dogfight. In the scratching matches of old, many a dog that would have lost a "street contest" went on to "out survive" its opponent. There were, and are, really hard hitters among the most famous pit dogs, but not all that many of the great dogs were especially hard hitters. They survived as much on heart as they did on muscle.

In any event, it is due to the above mentioned that I have observed a change in the Pit Bull breed, on the whole, with regard to both form and function. The process of selection for Pit Bulls being born today is not the same as it was when virtually every Pit Bull born came from the yard of a serious pit fighter. Again, don't get me wrong here. Many good, game-bred Pit Bulls are still being born today and with a little research, they can be made readily available to you. (Don't call me. I don't recommend breeders!) But whereas once virtually

The rare beer-drinking variety of the American Pit Bull Terrier,
photographed in the home of Heineken and Amstel, Amsterdam,
a city the author remembers fondly!

all Pit Bulls were good, sound, game-bred dogs, today a
minority of these dogs is bred by people who are making an
effort to preserve the definitive qualities of this breed. This
is a very unfortunate situation indeed. The game-bred dogs
still possess a much more stable temperament and so create
less trouble for the breed. Game dogmen today won't have a
man-biting dog in their yard, and many don't want to hear
about a dog over 50 pounds, if that. These dogs also look like
what a pit dog is supposed to look like and thus, it is these
dogs which preserve the appearance, as well as the character,
of this fine breed. It's odd, isn't it, that if one sincerely wants
a good pit dog that will not be a liability to its owner today,
one is best securing a pup from a game dog breeder's yard?

Before leaving the matter of variation in type among
Pit Bulls, I would like to make a minor departure from the
somewhat "general information" mode that we have been in

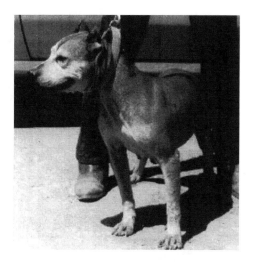

The last known daughter of Davis's
Boomerang, this is Miss Boomerang.
The Jazzman bought this dog
from Bert Sorrell and bred her to
Grand Champion Bad Billy, another
descendant of Boomerang.

so far and instead, speak, for a moment, to the real student of the breed. I must tell you that the following is information that I would undoubtedly have thought about, but not discussed, had it not been for an unusual group of men I found myself involved with recently.

We have heard a great deal about "the information superhighway" or "the Internet." All matters related to computers, but especially the state of the art, "really in demand" stuff, like the Internet, are changing so quickly that I realize as I am writing this, how antiquated it will sound years from now, to those of you who are reading this book then. But today, bear in mind, that ready availability home access to the Internet is brand new, and possibly the single most exciting thing to have happened to those in search of

This bitch is called Bambi. She lives in Perth, Australia. and produced a highly game Bandog named Cujo.

any information, ever. It is possibly the greatest tool ever developed by man.

At present, there are some 20 to 30 million people, worldwide, who access the Internet regularly. I am one of them. These people are interested in anything and everything you can possibly imagine, including game dogs! Due to the sensitivity of this particular subject, the group which discusses game dogs openly, is a closed group. In order to be part of the discussion, one must be approved by the group. I am a member of this group. (Please don't ask me to help you join the group, because I will not.)

We "talk dogs" in this group, and because all of the members in the group are always right there, in my computer, I can talk dogs any time I care to. As such, things come to mind that I will bounce off the members of this group casually. On occasion, I am very surprised that some members

Although this dog lives in Germany, he resembles a lot of famous old dogs from America's fighting past.

agree with what others might think is a very far-out idea. My idea about the range in Pit Bull type was one idea that I was surprised to find enthusiastic agreement with. As such, I became interested enough in my own idea, to mention it to you now. (Thanks, Cyberspace Dogmen!)

Even before the recent explosion in popularity of the Pit Bull breed, there was a noticeable range in type among Pit Bulls. This is not to suggest that the Pit Bull was not a homogeneous breed, mind you. It was every bit as homogeneous as any of the world's finest purebreds are. But within any breed, there is a range in type, and it is the responsibility of those who would understand the breed to understand why this range exists.

In the case of the Pit Bull there are at least three indicators of variability in type of those game-bred dogs of days gone by,

A sporting Pit Bull from Germany.

as well as of today. One indicator is size. Some Pit Bull lines are typically larger than others (and I am not talking about dogs of the past two decades here either). Another indicator is ear shape and size (obviously, on dogs that have not been cropped). Some Pit Bulls have smaller, thicker, more likely to be "rose-shaped" ears, while others have larger, not as thick, floppier ears. A third indicator is fighting style. Some Pit Bulls are born to be chest or stifle dogs, while others are born to be ear dogs. This is to say that in combat, some Pit Bulls will naturally seek an ear, or a jowl hold first. Among these, some will keep this hold until the opponent begins to run out of energy, and then go for a more devastating hold, while some will continue with the ear. As an aside here, a dog that seeks to establish and then to continue with an ear hold, is not generally a winning dog, as game as it may be. This is due to the fact that tearing an ear will not kill a dog or hurt it seriously. Breaking its leg, or crushing its chest, is another matter.

Ared-nosed red dog from Germany
who is being kept nice and lean.
Owners may find, as the author has,
that walking a dog to keep the pounds
off can benefit both walker and walkee.

But, be this as it may, there is disagreement among dogmen as to whether this is learned behavior or genetics. To my mind, this is a closed, decided matter. Ear dogs are born type of the most typical representatives of this breed.

I think I have the answer to this question. Like the American Bulldog, the Pit Bull was commonly bred for two purposes. One of these purposes was dogfighting, the other catch work. To make a long story short, the larger size of some bull-ear dogs. Their interest in taking the ear hold is an atavistic one. It seeks the ear because its very being tells it to. There is no conscious thought involved. But what do larger vs. smaller body size, big, floppy ears vs. smaller, tighter ears, and the genetic inclination of a pit dog to take one hold over another have to do with the history of this breed? This is the

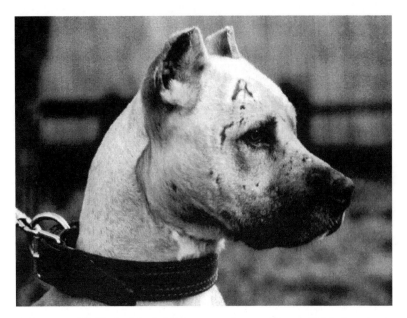

A German Pit Bull with tightly cropped ears. Doesn't this boy look like he's been around the block a few times?

question we must answer if we are to understand the range in dogs renders them more suitable for catch work, and in fact these larger dogs are often referred to by game-dog fanciers as being of "catch weight." The predisposition to go for the ear is classic catchdog strategy. A catchdog grabs an ear, or a jowl, but preferably an ear, and it holds that ear until its prey is totally exhausted. The globular ear, as opposed to the smaller, tighter ear, is typical of larger breeds that ranch raised Pit Bulls may have been crossed to at various times in the past in order to render a given line of hog-working Pit Bulls more suitable for catchwork.

Consider the qualities of a good old-time working American Bulldog and compare the very qualities that we have just been considering to the appearance and inclination of a working American Bull. The American Bull of old was larger, but not dramatically larger, than a Pit Bull. The American Bull typically sports longer, more globular ears as well, probably from some Mollossoid admixture in the past. And the working, American Bull, catchdog is an ear dog.

Pit Bull head over heels in protection work!

I think the above explains the range in type among pure, old-time, game-stock, Pit Bulls. I suppose we might want to look at Pit Bull tail length and thickness in addition to the above, as this might also be a meaningful indicator of "pure stock" range in type, but I think the case is made with consideration of ears, overall size, and hold inclination. But is there something additional to be learned, using this

195

information, not only about the range in type among Pit Bulls but about the relationship between the Pit Bull and the American Bulldog as well? Are larger ear-dog Pit Bulls an outcross to American Bull lines of old? Or possibly are there no true American Bull lines of old, and might it not simply be that the American Bull is a Pit Bull that has been outcrossed to some Molossian breeds in order to create a more suitable catchdog? This is a matter we'll save for another time. For now, the question on the table is the range of Pit Bull type, and the above are some of my observations and a conclusion that I have arrived at as a result of having made these observations. What's your thinking on this matter?

Anyway, I have said it before and I will say it again here. The Pit Bull is my favorite breed. This is not to say that these are the greatest dogs in the world, but instead, that they, for whatever reasons, appeal to me the most. For the truly curious, who would like to know what it is I like so much about Pit Bulls, let me try to explain. I remember once, while on live television, in front of a huge studio audience, I was asked this question. My answer was, 'This is a great breed. These dogs will love you." The audience responded with the kind of groan that means nothing but, 'This boy is clearly sick! He thinks these dogs love him." In the meantime, when I heard this response, what was going on in my mind was "How in the world did these television people find an entire audience of people who are so ignorant about dogs as not to understand what mankind has always known, which is that a good dog is man's best friend?"

A well-bred (game-bred) Pit Bull should be an easy-to-care-for, extremely loyal, thinking family dog that will bond closely to its human family. Biting people should not be something that it is inclined to do. It should be a useful defense dog only when its family is threatened, and then it should be able to think the situation through for itself and respond only when it knows that a physical response is the only thing left to do. It should never bite people for any reason. In fact, many highly game-bred dogs will even ignore other dogs on the street, displaying no outward signs of aggression toward any dog that is not displaying aggression toward it. Many will argue that this kind of behavior is too much to ask for from a dog and that dogs like this are very few and far between. These are the people who don't know the Pit Bull breed and who undoubtedly know very little about dogs in general.

Pit Bulls are a strong and determined dog—the most. This Pit Bull is being baited to pull a cart on a track.
Hard work for a hard dog.

Schaller's Champ lives and works in Germany. He is one of the few Am Staffs working in search and rescue.

AMERICAN
STAFFORDSHIRE
TERRIER

To some extent, the direction taken by breeders of the American Staffordshire Terrier has paralleled the direction taken by "novice" Pit Bull breeders over the course of the last decade. Because many newcomers to the Pit Bull breed were a little disappointed to learn that some of the toughest dogs around did not sport the large size, heavy bone, overly broad heads, etc., of the show-variety Am Staff. "When the truth be told," since these same newcomers were more interested in a dog that looked tough than one that actually was tough, they opted to impress their friends and neighbors with an Am Staff rather than to silently rest assured that they had the toughest dog on the block, in spite of outward appearance to the contrary.

What these people found was that while the American Staffordshire Terrier had not been game bred for a long time, and so was not competitive (on average, best against best) with the Pit Bull, it was still an impressive, powerful, devoted, tough, and good-looking little dog. For all practical purposes, those who opted for Am Staffs had all the benefits of Pit Bull ownership and some good, flashy looks as well. To further complicate matters, windows of opportunity opened during a period of time in which the American Kennel Club (which registers the Am Staff), and the United Kennel Club (which, along with the American Dog Breeder's Association, registers the Pit Bull) agreed to allow the dual registry of these dogs. In other words, some dogs were registered as Pit Bulls and Am Staffs. How was a novice to understand what was going on?

The novice didn't really care what was going on. Whether he or she got a dog that was registered as a Pit Bull or an Am Staff, or both, the dog was powerful, looked impressive, and was generally loyal to the core. The word spread among novices that these dogs were everything a person in search of a tough dog was looking for, and more and more novices flocked to the breed. As they came to the breed, they brought with them the preconceived ideas some of which were well founded, and some of which were not. One idea they brought with them in their search for a Pit Bull/Am Staff was that these dogs were broad and powerful-looking. To some extent, this was true. While the game-bred Pit Bull was never (typically) an especially broadly built, super powerful looking dog, the Am Staff had already been taken

Protection training with an Am Staff, conducted by Thomas
Kohlhoefer of Germany.

Tough Guy's Agapi is a handsome
Am Staff living in Austria.

in this direction by its breeders, many of whom were also, essentially, novices. As such, many a newcomer to the Pit Bull/Am Staff breed opted to purchase the more powerful-looking of the two dogs, the Am Staff.

The novices also bought with them the idea that the Pit Bull/Am Staff should be an outwardly aggressive and

202

Quasar vom Hungener Schloss, owned
by Peter Schwab of Switzerland.

particularly a "man-aggressive" dog. In this belief, they were
wrong. In the days before the explosion in Pit Bull popularity
took place, these dogs actually had the reputation of being too
docile for protection work! The Pit Bull was never, really, a
docile breed, but it was a breed that had no particular interest
in being outwardly aggressive toward man, and often it was a
dog that wasn't especially outwardly aggressive toward other
non-threatening dogs.

This disappointed many of the novices who rarely, if ever,
needed an aggressive dog, but who very much wanted a dog
that would frighten those around them. It would be nice if
I could tell you that these novices simply made themselves
look silly, and then they went away, but this isn't what
happened. What did happen was that they sent the message
to the dogs they bought, that outward aggression was what
they expected of their pets. In response to this, the individual

203

An athletic, enthusiastic animal, Tough Guy's Bullet, bred and owned by Guenther Haas of Austria.

Pit Bull/Am Staff, being a dog that aims to please, often managed to make itself outwardly aggressive.

Worse than this, however, is the fact that Am Staff breeders soon realized that large, thick, aggressive Am Staffs were what "the audience" wanted. All kinds of people got involved in Am Staff breeding. People got involved who would eventually brag to me that their champion stud dog, who himself had been beaten enough so that it would no longer lunge at show judges and other strangers, had produced puppies that would attack a man with intent to kill at five months of age. One breeder bragged to me that her normally gentile stud dog had broken through its kennel one evening, tore open the kennels of five other dogs in the room, and killed each. Great! Just what you want to sell to some unsuspecting family that thinks it wants a tough dog.

Old-time game-bred Pit Bulls didn't do things like this, and most modern show-bred, American Staffordshire

Tough Guy's Colby (that name rings
a bell somehow?), bred by Guenther
Haas and owned by Gerhard Shawki.
This is not the first Am Staff connected
with the name Colby. John P. Colby
dual-registered lots of dogs as Am
Staffs with the AKC and Pit Bulls with
the UKC.

Terriers don't either, but the trend in breeding modern Pit
Bulls and Staffs as well is toward breeding a larger, thicker
dog with temperamental qualities that are not typical of the
breed. Some are as docile as lambs under all circumstances
as a result of selective breeding for these qualities. While
this may be better than producing dangerous dogs, it is not a
quality that is typical of the breed. Some are overly aggressive

Austria seems like an interesting place for an Am Staff to live.

practices, poor ownership, and perhaps poor breeding as well, and this is not what this breed was only a few years ago either. Some are just fine, and if you find one, you are sure to have a great dog.

Today's American Staffordshire Terrier is often a truly handsome dog. While a 60-pound dog once defined the upper end of the weight range for males, an 80-pound dog is not uncommon in the show-ring today. These dogs are thick, square, and hard. Their heavy bone structure supports what looks to be nothing but muscle. There is no denying that they are impressive.

Neither is there any denying that dogs like this did exist in history. But exactly as I said of the Pit Bull breed, dogs like this never defined the breed, as they do today. Oddly, I find myself watching American Staffordshire Terriers showing today and while once I thought, "There's all the dog a man needs in a very manageable package," today I think,

Quasar vom Hungener Schloss, bred by Thomas Kohlhoefer, enjoys the reputation of being the best protection dog in Switzerland.

Schwab's Mickey trying to remove a piece of agitator Thomas Kohlhoefer's left arm.

Thomas Kohlhoefer, breeder and agitator, run an Am Staffclub in Germany, dedicated to producing sound working dogs. They are less concerned with conformation and concentrate on functional ability.

Fire, a ten-year-old Am Staff bitch owned by Thomas Kohlhoefer, is a well-trained protection dog whose age doesn't seem to detract from her performance.

Frankie Capodiferro with Tarzan, owned by mom Eloise Capodiferro of California, good friends of the author. Tarzan is one good-looking Am Staff and a fine family dog too.

"It's nice to look at, but it's more dog than a man needs." As I am writing this, I am not sure how much of this feeling reflects changes in me and how much reflects changes in the American Staffordshire Terrier as a breed. Whatever the answer to this question is, I am sure that these dogs are changing and that the changes we see are not in the direction of making these dogs even more typical of what this breed once was, but rather less typical.

If I were "King of the Dog Show," which I will never be, here is the advice that I would give those who view themselves as being qualified to judge Am Staffs. I would tell these people to examine historical photographs of Pit Bulls that lived before 1970. I would tell them to pay special attention to the photographs of those Pit Bulls of pit-winning acclaim and of pit-winning heritage. I would remind these judges that the goal of the dog show is to preserve what we found in its purest form, and not to create our own ideal or to satisfy someone else's erroneous ideal. I would remind them, if not inform them, that the written breed standard assumes that those who will study it have a knowledge of dogs and of breed history. When a standard says that a head or chest of a breed should be "broad," this does not mean that we can abandon common sense and that the broadest is the best. It assumes that a judge has an understanding of breed history and realizes that the word "broad" should be reasoned in relative as opposed to absolute terms.

I would also remind judges, that character is even more important than cosmetics in judging a breed like the American Staffordshire Terrier, and that a dog that is brainless and unresponsive to its owner is a dog of zero value. A judge should do a bit of reading, as well as picture viewing, and come to understand why the people who owned this dog in history loved it so much. Any would-be representative of this breed that doesn't establish and maintain eye contact with its owner at all times while in the ring is of suspicious character, and in my opinion, may be atypical of this fine breed.

In conclusion, let me tell you that the American Staffordshire Terrier, in its purest form, is as fine a dog as lives today, or that has ever lived. But as much as I might like to, I cannot pick your family's puppy for you. This job is yours. I advise you to do it well.

STAFFORDSHIRE
BULL
TERRIER

T he story of the Staffordshire Bull Terrier is an interesting one which gets more interesting all the time. Before getting into the details of the breed, I'd like to say a few words about the politics of the breed, as the politics of this breed offers us great insight into the establishment of legislation and the value of some legislation once it has been enacted.

With the passage of legislation prohibiting the new acquisition of and the breeding of the American Pit Bull Terrier breed throughout the United Kingdom, dog fighters throughout England, and to some extent throughout the

Grand Champion Big Red is a line example of a pure Dublin Red Staffy Bull from England today. Big Red is extremely game and athletic and weighs 47 pounds and stands 20 inches tall, which is pretty large for a game-bred Staffy Bull. Even the Pit Bull fraternity should be impressed by a dog this athletic! Photograph courtesy of Mick Tate.

United Kingdom, renewed their interest in the Staffordshire Bull Terrier. The reason for this renewed interest in "Staff Bulls" was, and is, that the Staff Bull and the Pit Bull are very similar breeds, maybe even more so than the supposedly identical breed, the American Staffordshire Terrier. The Staffordshire Bull Terrier has, as a breed, retained a great deal of the temperamental qualities that are found in, and that are most typical of, the finest Pit Bulls of all time.

For the benefit of those who have not read my first book and who are otherwise unfamiliar with this breed, the Staffordshire Bull Terrier is the small bull and terrier

A four-month-old game-bred Stafford
shire Bull Terrier pup with a lurcher
(a greyhound-like hunting dog).
Photograph courtesy of Mick Tate.

fighting dog of England that was originally brought to the United States, giving rise to the American Pit Bull Terrier breed. No other breed was added to these original English bloodlines to produce the American Pit Bull Terrier, and the current differences between the two breeds are the result of selective breeding in America being different than the selective breeding of Staffordshire Bulls throughout the UK.

Unlike the American Staffordshire Terrier, which is simply a Pit Bull that has been bred purely for show purposes, the Staffordshire Bull was bred (in modern times), and still is

213

bred, mostly for show, but sometimes for working purposes. The working use of the Staff Bull in modern years has been primarily "going to ground" for badger and other game, as opposed to pit fighting, but going to ground is a grueling sport which requires immense courage, tenacity, and overall physical ability, and as such, the Staff Bull has retained a great deal in the way of these qualities.

Dog fighters in the UK today will tell you that the Staffordshire Bull Terrier, even from the gamest lines, is not sufficiently competitive with the Pit Bull. But they will also tell you that sufficiently competitive or not, these are highly game dogs which are improving steadily in the area of gameness. Some report that gameness is being improved purely by game testing the best of the Staff Bulls in the UK and selectively breeding only the gamest stock. Others report that legislation against Pit Bulls notwithstanding, highly game Pit Bulls are still in, and still finding their way into, the UK and being used in Staff Bull breeding programs. One acquaintance of mine reports that a fine dog of his, Grand Champion Badger, a 35-pound, highly game and serious-winning Pit Bull dog, currently resides in Ireland, in fact, and it is more than coincidental that many of today's best young Staff Bulls look much like this game little American dog. Still others report, and there is no doubt that this is true, though not a very widespread practice, that many a game little dog is being produced in the UK by crossing Staffordshire Bulls to the English Bull Terrier.

The point here is that the UK has now strapped itself with another utterly useless law when the anti-dogfighting legislation that already existed would have been perfectly adequate, had it only been enforced. Now responsible Pit

The author's son Alex with two of
Tony George's Staffy Bulls. From New
York City, Tony has been shaking
things up by doing his homework and
producing dogs that look and act more
athletic than your average show-ring
Staffordshire Bull Terrier.

Bull owners, who had no desire to match their dogs, but who
preferred to keep their dogs purely as family pets, have been
penalized and can no longer own their favorite breed, while
those who had no regard for the earlier laws, and similarly
have no regard for current laws, continue to do precisely
what they had been doing all along.

Some will argue that the anti-Pit Bull ordinance put
in place in the UK was not principally about dogfighting,

215

An English show-bred Staffy Bull at nine months of age.

but rather it was about public safety. In fact, when I was in Birmingham, England, shortly before the anti-Pit Bull ordinance was effected, to appear on television to discuss the matter of Pit Bulls with members of Parliament, representatives of RSPCA, and others. The subject of primary concern was definitely the damage that a Pit Bull could potentially do to passing children (as if hurting children was something that a well-raised Pit Bull was more likely to do than other breeds). My point stands and it is that if a game-bred Pit Bull is likely to hurt someone because it possesses not only the physical ability necessary to do so but also a powerful "prey drive" and a naturally aggressive nature, then certainly a Staffordshire Bull Terrier that is essentially the same dog, and that is just as game bred, will be just as potentially dangerous. As such, the breed-specific law against the Pit Bull alone will not help the "dangerous dog" situation there, or elsewhere.

Staffy Bull bred by Tony George, playing with his two-foot length of four by four, which he sometimes carries around the yard in his mouth . . . for an hour!

Well, legislation notwithstanding, I am a huge fan of the Staffordshire Bull Terrier, as a breed, game bred or otherwise. In the United States, Staffordshire Bull Terrier breeding stock is purely show stock but somehow these little show dogs have managed to retain much of the character that originally defined the breed. Perhaps, as in the case of many smaller dogs, the reason for this is that the Staff Bull was never viewed as being large enough to do serious damage to a person (as the American Staffordshire Terrier was), and so the spirit of the breed was never quite as suppressed by fearful breeders. These are intelligent little dogs with "bubbly personalities" and a strong attachment to their human family. They are also generally regarded as a fine dog for children, and I have never known one that did not fit this description. They do tend to be a little energetic though, and anyone who isn't interested in owning a little dog that may, at times, see fit to fly around the house like a little rocketship, cutting comers around the legs of the kitchen table as if it was bolted

217

The author making friends with a cute show-bred Staffy Bull pup
named Amigo, owned by the author's long-time friend,
Chris Ariola.

to a track and stuck on high speed may want to find a slightly more "subdued" breed.

These days, the Staffordshire Bull Terrier is not quite as small as many imagine either. Efforts to increase the size of this breed are being made in the US as well as in England. Even in the American show circuit it is not uncommon to see well-put-together male Staffordshire Bulls tipping the scale at 50 pounds or better, and in England many of the most serious game dogmen are complaining that this breed is getting too large, primarily in response to what others see as being a need to recreate the Pit Bull which was banned.

Once again, I think the Staffordshire Bull Terrier demonstrates another example of how and why we can thank the game dogman for having preserved a breed in its working form, and how this working form renders this breed the ideal companion dog for many homes. This is a loyal dog, and normally a very trustworthy dog, for a home with children. This is a small dog, and yet one that possesses such incredible strength that its determination to defend its home, family and its family's property is far out of proportion with its bulky, yet diminutive, size. This is an easy to care for (low maintenance) breed. And this is a breed that will relax when its family is relaxed and which, when the occasion arises, can display high energy like the world of human beings would hardly think possible.

I love the Staff Bull, and to those who are inclined to own a dog for the family, a well-bred, responsibly raised Staffordshire Bull Terrier can easily become one of those dogs that will dominate the family's photo album, and find its way into your family's history. This is not a dog for the dog fighter who is intent upon winning, but it may well be a fine dog for the sporting dogman, and is certainly a breed of choice for a companion and family dog. Consider it, if you are serious about owning a very "real" dog.

BULL
TERRIER

On the American scene, the Bull Terrier is one example of a breed that has not changed very much over the course of the past decade. The breed was good for what it was good for when I wrote *The World of Fighting Dogs* and it is just as good now. Essentially, these dogs are fun family dogs and, as such, they make good pets. Owners of good Bull Terriers love the breed and tend to stay with it when their old dog succumbs to the passage of time. These dogs are of no interest to the sporting-dog crowd, and this is as things should remain, unless someone, somewhere, is willing to invest a great deal of work in resurrecting this breed to its original form.

Friar Tuck's Lancer, bred and owned by Rudolf Sewerin of Germany. Any doubt that Rudolf's Bull Terriers (like all his dogs) are functional working dogs?

The Bull Terrier was originally developed as a fighting dog, and was quickly adopted by those who wanted to watch a game-bred terrier kill vast numbers of rats in the shortest time possible in the rat pits of days gone by. It was also quickly adopted as a pet dog, and the fact that it has been a pet for so long may account for its success in this area.

But while those who know the Bull Terrier and who love the breed are content with this dog as a pet, newcomers to the breed are sometimes disappointed, and the reasons for their disappointment should be understood before the decision is made to bring one of these puppies home. The sporting history of the breed, combined with its bizarre appearance,

There's no denying that Bull Terriers
are good-looking dogs. These dogs
have always been favorites of Dr.
Semencic's.

can easily draw one's attention to these dogs. I know that it
did mine, very early on. I'll never forget the first Bull Terrier
I ever saw. It was a large white male, walking down the street
with its owner. When I stopped dead in my tracks in awe of
the solid dog that was walking by, its owner was more than
willing to offer information about the breed and its history,
as well as to simply "chat dogs." I remember walking away
from that conversation determined to have a dog like that

Above and below: Two Bull Terriers bred and owned by Peet and Nonnie Oosthuizen of Somerset Wes, South Africa. The colored BT is Piketberg Entire Magic and the white BT is Champion Piketberg Trois Fire n Ice.

some day. It's sometimes strange how chance encounters can affect a person.

Too often, prospective Bull Terrier owners will come to the breed from other breeds, with ideas concerning what the Bull Terrier should be like. Too often this isn't what the Bull Terrier is like at all, and this is where the disappointment comes in. For example, many prospective Bull Terrier owners are either Pit Bull owners, former Pit Bull owners, or people who otherwise know the Pit Bull breed, but prefer the Bull Terrier's "look." They are disappointed when they learn what a very different dog the Bull Terrier is than is the Pit Bull.

To be perfectly blunt, the Bull Terrier is often an awfully knuckle-headed breed compared to the Pit Bull and other (working) bull breeds. The kind of responsiveness that those who have owned a good Pit Bull have come to expect of a dog is largely absent in the Bull Terrier breed. While the Pit Bull is a breed that will always come to you when you call it, the Bull Terrier is not. While the Pit Bull is a dog that will become completely devoted to its master, the Bull Terrier is a dog that will often walk off with a stranger if the stranger is friendly and the walk seems like fun to the dog. How serious an offense either of these attributes is viewed as is really a matter of perspective. Whereas those who know the breed might view the Bull Terrier's comical desire to run and play with anyone who will have him to be a positive quality, those who wanted a dog that was likely to bond with its owner more closely will be offended, and disappointed, by this kind of behavior.

I have mentioned this attitude to many Bull Terrier breeders and time and time again they admit that, "Well, they're terriers, after all." But then, the Pit Bull is a terrier

Dr. Semencic met this Bushman (Kung) family while visiting South Africa. The Oosthuizens explained that it is the woman's responsibility to care for the dogs. This family lives on the Oosthuizens' five-acre estate.

too, admittedly with less terrier in it than the Bull Terrier. Pure terriers tend to display more of the attitude so often found in the Bull Terrier, and possibly this additional terrier blood renders these dogs much more terrier-like than either the Pit Bull Terrier or the Staffordshire Bull Terrier. I tend to feel that there is something else going on here as well.

The problem with this "Well, it's a terrier" attitude is that I clearly recall more responsive, closer bonding Bull Terriers from the past. Furthermore, the occasional "good" (from my perspective) Bull Terrier still crops up among modern Bull Terriers. It has been my observation that if a modern Bull Terrier is going to be a responsive dog, chances are that it will be colored as opposed to white, and that it will not be a dog which demonstrates the exaggerated physical type that attracts so many of us, myself included, to the breed in the first place. For the benefit of those Bull Terrier owners and

Nonnie Oosthuizen with a large litter of BT pups. Eleven is a large litter for this medium-sized breed. The author is grateful to Nonnie and her husband Peet for the hospitality they extended toward him on his visit to their kennel.

readers who do not have any idea what I am talking about, let me tell you that I mentioned this observation of mine to at show breeder of Bull Terriers that are used for obedience work as well and this breeder, who will remain nameless agreed wholeheartedly. In the breeder's opinion the Bull Terrier will generally never be as responsive to command and attentive to its owner as the American Staffordshire Terrier or the Pit Bull. If one does find a responsive Bull Terrier, it is very likely to be a small brindle bitch.

Be this as it may, the Bull Terrier, in spite of the breed's working history, is rarely used as a working dog of any kind in the United States. It has been ages since these dogs were game-bred as fighting dogs or as dogs for going to ground. They are not well liked by protection-dog trainers because once made aggressive, they too often become irresponsibly aggressive. I have seen really good working Bull Terriers, but these dogs are few and far between. In Germany the Bull Terrier is used as a protection dog quite often and many have excelled at this task. In England, Bull Terriers are being crossed into Staffordshire Bull Terrier lines (especially since the ban of the Pit Bull) to produce an effective working dog for badger hunting and lately for organized fighting as well. Reports I've received claim that the Bull Terrier can be very effective as a "working" dog, even today, when careful attention is paid to selective breeding.

But in the United States, no attention has been paid to the breeding of working Bull Terriers, and as a result, this is a breed for the pet owner who likes this kind of dog. On a positive note, if this is your kind of dog, there is a great deal to like in a good Bull Terrier. This is a sweet, fun-loving happy breed. They have as much energy to use at play as any dog has and yet they are a dog that can play the part of "couch potato" very well when the time comes to relax. I wouldn't say that the Bull Terrier is a prime choice for use as a children's dog, but for the careful, prospective owner, a well-bred Bull Terrier can fit into a household with children just fine. Play between any dog, the Bull Terrier included, and children, should always be supervised, and rough housing should be discouraged.

I suppose it isn't a bad thing that the Bull Terrier breed has stayed the same as it has been in the United States, but it might have been nice if some attention had been paid to the overall character of this breed, in addition to its temperament and its looks. I believe that it would be a worthwhile goal for someone in this country to produce a Bull Terrier that responds to human command like a Pit Bull does. I suspect the attitude that would be produced from this effort would be more typical of the breed, in its original form, than the attitude we so commonly see in Bull Terriers today.

Seven-month-old male white BT
named Eugen Ironheart and a colored
BT are owned by Zukova Tanya of
Russia.

Above, below and facing page: Schutzhund work undertaken by trainer and Bull Terriers in Germany. When trained for protection, Bull Terriers prove to be competent guardians.

Above: Viola, a BT bitch from Germany, owned by Mike Abelski.
Below: Champion Piketberg Top Dhu Drop, owned and bred by
Peet and Nonnie Oosthuizen.

Champion Piketberg Ideal Topdrawer and Piketberg Ideal Tune with breeder Nonnie Oosthuizen. The author was struck by the massive bone on these dogs. Piketberg kennels is probably the largest BT breeding establishment in South Africa.

Chamption Piketberg Top Talk O Town.

Champion Piketberg Ideal Dixieonze.

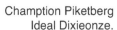

AMERICAN
BULLDOG

I must tell you that I have been looking forward to writing this chapter. The primary reason for this anticipation on my part is that, more than any other breed to be discussed here, the current condition of the American Bulldog gives meaning and purpose to this book. Remember, my goal in writing this book is to bring those who read *The World of Fighting Dogs*, published in 1984, up to speed. The condition of the American Bulldog, as a breed, has changed very dramatically since then and readers have some very serious catching up.

In order to understand how much this breed has changed over the past two decades, it will be helpful to understand where it was two decades ago. I will tell you where it was then,

Aaron Dial's Br'er Dog Chase, co-owned by Aaron and Sheila Dial, out of Jack Osgood's breeding. The author met Chase when the dog was very young and before he acquired such awesome musculature in his rear and shoulders. Jack Osgood continues to produce some very fine dogs!

because it was 1974 when I began to seriously investigate this breed, and so I am in a position to know where it was. At that time, investigation demanded not that one read about the breed, because there was virtually nothing to read, but that one pick up the telephone and make long-distance phone calls wherever possible to talk to the few breeders of American Bulldogs (then called American Pit Bull Dogs), and to take any opportunity to visit a home that contained an American Bulldog in order to get an idea what it was the people on the other end of the phone were talking about.

I must warn you at this point that, for whatever reason, many of today's American Bulldog breeders will deny that so few American Bulldogs existed such a short time ago. Many will make lofty claims about having been breeders of these dogs before *The World of Fighting Dogs* was published.

Chuck Koura with Rode Hawg Bella
Boo (out of Belle Star by Bandit), a
bitch that ideally combines good looks
and working ability. She is a good,
steady, protective family dog.

I suggest that in order to confirm that what I am telling you is accurate, what you should do is to check issues of the major dog magazines which have numerous ads for American Bulldogs today. Then look at issues from the 1970s, and onward, and take a look at who was advertising American Bulldog puppies for sale. I'll tell you what you will find. Nobody was. In fact, what you will find is that the first mention of the American Bulldog in any of the major dog magazines (and in any magazine, anywhere, with the exception of one magazine to be discussed below) was an article by me. I called it "Introducing the American Bulldog."

Larry Koura's Max Dog. The Rode
Hawg kennels breeds performance-
oriented active Bulldogs, never
bending toward the current aesthetic
trends in breeding.

The ads began after that article was published. The first
Bulldog breeder to advertise, and an old timer in the breed
to be sure, was the man I discussed in my article. I think it is
important to understand this, because understanding it will
help to serve as an explanation for how it is that this breed
is expressed in so many different forms today. Furthermore,
this is an important part of American Bulldog history now,
and those who would know the Bulldog should know its real
history.

In the early 1970s there was one little-read stockman's
publication put out by a family-run registry organization
known as The Animal Research Foundation (or the ARF)
out of Quinlan, Texas, which offered the podium to the

Patch was a 75-pound bitch and the beloved companion of Michael Harlow, author of *K-9 Bodyguards*. She is heavily featured in that book, showing off her superiorworking ability.Mike says that Patch was "hard as Chinese arithmetic!"

few Southerners who kept, bred, and used the American Bulldog. The founder of the organization was a man named Tom Stodghill. Along with letters and articles by just anyone who felt like writing in about a variety of dogs and assorted livestock, there was the occasional letter/article and, not in every issue but often enough, a few ads for "American Pit Bull Dogs" (not to be confused with the American Pit Bull Terrier). I quickly became interested in these dogs because at that time, I owned a large 66-pound, pure-white, black-nosed American Pit Bull Terrier and what I saw in the ads

A Screaming Eagle bitch who lives in America's last frontier, Alaska. This Bulldog kennel produces dogs at the upper end of the scale and no bigger: bitches 60 to 80 pounds, dogs 80 to 100 pounds.

in this stockman's publication reminded me of a somewhat larger version of my dog.

I can still recall one of the first telephone conversations I ever had with a breeder of American Bulldogs. This very well-known dogman, and certainly one of the few alive whom we can think of as being primarily responsible for saving this breed from what certainly appeared to be the imminent extinction (because there were so few breeders and there was so little interest), responded to my inquiry about American Bulldogs with two questions. The first question was, "Are you sure you're interested in the American Pit Bulldog and not the Pit Terrier?" I assured him that I was well aware of what a Pit Bull Terrier was and that it was an American Pit

Like the American Bulldog, the Black mouthed Cur is used for catchwork. This all-American country dog, owned by Jerry Briffa of Brooklyn, is a shining example of this protective, aggressive propertyguard.The movie "Old Yeller" features a Black-mouth Cur.

Bulldog that I was interested in. His second question was, "Are you looking for a short-faced one or a long-faced one?" I asked him if he bred two lines which were distinct with regard to length of face and he responded, "No. They come out of the same litters." I then asked him how big a large mature American Pit Bulldog was. He informed me that a large male would often weigh as much as 85 pounds, females to about 70 or 75 pounds. He went on to tell me that the color of these dogs was generally white.

You might find it curious that I viewed the American Pit Bull Dog of the early 1970s as being so similar to my 66-pound American Pit Bull Terrier, and well you should. After all, to look at the ads depicting giant, incredibly heavy boned, bully-beyond-belief American Bulldogs in the magazines today, you wouldn't think that anyone interested in the smaller, finer boned, more athletic Pit Bull would care for these very different dogs. The interesting fact is, however, that only two decades ago the average American Pit Bull Dog and a rather large, white Pit Bull Terrier, like mine, were not nearly as far apart, with regard to their conformation, as they are today.

This description of the American Pit Bulldog of the mid-1970s was in keeping with the appearance of the dogs from the yards of other bulldog breeders that I had seen in pictures in the ARF journals. These were not very large dogs though they were athletic dogs. More often than not they were not a very short-faced dog, but rather they sported a longer, but thick, working muzzle. They were often white with some dark markings. The tails of these dogs were longer, thicker, and more "feathered" than that of a Pit Bull. All the dogs being advertised were from the Southeast, most from Georgia and Alabama. Oddly, though they were a working Bulldog and being advertised in a stockman's magazine, no one at the time spoke about hog catching. Possibly this was due to the fact that they knew they were speaking with a New Yorker who would have no use for a catch dog, but great use for a guard dog and possible use for a fighting dog.

If you will look at the photographs provided in my first book *The World of Fighting Dogs*, you will notice that most of the dogs pictured were not exceptionally large, but some were. To look at these early pictures of large Bulldogs, one would not expect that a top breeder, only a few years before, would have described a large male a being an 85-pound dog. One can see, in the pictures provided in *The World of Fighting*

Dogs as well as in the numerous display ads in the magazines of today, that muzzle length was variable among Bulldogs. It still is.

In *The World of Fighting Dogs* I told my readers that I didn't really know what these dogs were, where they had come from, or when. I said that I was sure that these dogs had been around for a long time, and I offered a photograph (of a Bull-dog) that was over 40 years old before the publication of *The World of Fighting Dogs*. I said I did not believe that these dogs were simply the Bulldog of Elizabethan England, imported to the United States early on and surviving here in their pure form. I said I thought they were created by crossing American Pit Bull Terrier, Bullmastiff, English Bulldog (show variety), and other breeds. Today, I have much more information to work with than I did then, and the good news is that I am surprised at how right I was about these dogs back then. The bad news is that I still don't know what the American Bulldog is, and I don't believe any man living does, or ever will, either. Let me tell you what I know, and what I think, about the American Bulldog.

First, we should recognize that the breed name has been officially changed. Mind you, I don't think there is anything official about the American Bulldog, but this completely unofficial status is a very large part of the breed's charm. There was some early denial that these dogs were ever used as fighting dogs, and one author went so far as to write a book in which she included a chapter on the American Bulldog, only mentioning my earlier work on the breed in order to state, unequivocally, that I was wrong about the fighting history of this breed. She did not bother to explain why the breed name had only recently been changed from

American Pit Bull Dog if it was not a fighting dog, but this is undoubtedly because she simply didn't know this about the American Bulldog.

The breed name was undoubtedly changed, during the early 1980s, not in order to be politically correct, but rather simply to avoid confusion with the American Pit Bull Terrier breed. The earlier breed name, combined with the fact that many older dogmen remember the American Bulldog as a pit fighter, and the fact that many modern dogmen know the American Bulldog as a fighter today, tells us that dogfighting was, and is, certainly one of the uses for which this breed was and is produced.

The American Bulldog serves as a guardian of the home, property (including livestock), and its human family as well, and this was one use of the breed that was impressed upon me when I first began to investigate the breed during the early 1970s. The breed serves well as a powerful protector of livestock from marauding packs of "wild" dogs and other predators on the farm, as well as a protector of suburban homes against human intruders.

The American Bulldog can also be a fine catch dog, and although this usage was not described to me during the 1970s, I would be very surprised to learn that this was not a common use for this breed at that time. In fact, I would go so far as to say that it is probable that catch work was the primary function of this breed during the time it was kept before its modern-day explosion in popularity. One contemporary breeder of Bulldogs, Bill Hines of Harlingen, Texas, sent me a video of a few of his Bulldogs being used in catch work, one of his 70-pound bitches having been featured in particular. The video was so impressive that no matter how many times

I watched it, I couldn't view the part in which the bitch hit the wild hog it had been set upon without getting a chill up my spine (literally). The video demonstrated that a good Bulldog, of the smaller working size, is an animal completely devoid of fear for its own well being. It also demonstrated how incredibly athletic a smaller working Bulldog can be.

But where did they come from and when? What is it that this breed is made of? Are they "purebred," in the sense of the word that we have come to understand? How has this breed changed, and why? These are the real questions, and I will answer them to the best of my ability. Again, however, the more I learn about this breed, the more convinced I become that it will remain clouded in uncertainty forever.

First, where did the Bulldog come from, and when? We know that they have been in the United States for a long time. Not only have I spoken with older people who remember their grandfathers talking about owning these dogs when they were young themselves, but photographs occasionally depict a dog which could very easily be a Bulldog. My mother owned a Bulldog as early as 1920. The fundamental question of exactly where the foundation stock that gave rise to the American Bulldog originally came from is the aspect of American Bulldog history that will never be answered. It is undoubtedly lost to us, unless someone, somewhere, has some family photos from days gone by that can help us to resolve this matter.

Is the initial stock, the foundation stock, of the American Bulldog, a few imported English dogs which themselves were leftovers from Elizabethan times? Not only do I doubt it, but frankly, it no longer makes any difference, because the crossbreeding that accounts for the existence of this breed

Petey with the author's uncle Frank Ingardiola, circa 1920.

Circa 1920, the author's grandmother, Maria Mannino Favorito, whom he never met, with Petey as a very young puppy. She had to bottlefeed him to keep him alive. Apparently she did well since he grew to be big and strong.

in its current form is so extensive as to render the question of foundation stock almost totally meaningless. That's right. These are crossbred dogs and it is extensive, widespread crossbreeding to other breeds which accounts for the fact that this breed has changed so dramatically, in size and in form, in such a short period of time, and the fact that today's stock is so widely divergent with regard to these same features.

Few breeders will discuss their breeding experiments openly, though some have discussed them with me. While I will not discuss them with anyone, we can discuss a few of the breeds that have gone into the breeding of American Bulldog stock in recent times. Some of the breeds to which the American Bulldog has been crossed during the past two decades are the Bullmastiff, Pit Bull, and modern-variety English Bulldog. This has been admitted in the form of showing the ancestry of many American Bulldogs as having sprung from Bullmeade's Queen (an Olde Bulldogge owned by David Leavitt), a dog of known parentage which was made of the breeds mentioned. But this is far from the only time that these breeds found their way into American Bulldog bloodlines.

The Chicago Bulldogs are known to have been crossed to the Pit Bull repeatedly in recent years, and the dogs out of Georgia are strongly suspected of having been bred to Bullmastiffs, and certainly to English Bulldogs.

The Georgia Bulldogs are also known to have been crossed to St. Bernards, and along with Bulldogs from other areas of the country, to the Catahoula Leopard Dog as well (a useful, rather than purely cosmetic cross at least). One breeder in Georgia no longer even refers to her dogs as American Bulldogs because they are composed of at least as

This rare photograph is important for historical reasons, but near to the author's heart as well. "That's my mom, pictured at age 15, with her Bulldog Petey. Mom died in 1994 at age 86, so this shot goes back a ways (like to 1923). As much as my mom talked about Petey and what a wonderful family dog he was (they had him for many years), I had never seen this picture. When I was about 20, I went out into the world to buy myself a dog, I came home with a pure white black-nosed Pit Bull (Nugget), just about Petey's size. This picture was taken on a street in Brooklyn and my mom was part of the old Sicilian population there during the 1920s. I used to ask my mom if Petey was a Pit Bull, and she would always say, "No, he was a Bulldog" (and she knew what a Pit Bull was, too!). These photographs may be the earliest representations of the American Bulldog ever published!

much Catahoula (or Louisiana Cat) as they are Bulldog, so some bogus, exotic name has been concocted for these dogs instead.

It is strongly suspected that the Plott Hound has found its way into American Bulldog lines, and I know for a fact that white Boxer has been added to the gene pool on more than one occasion. How about longhaired English Mastiff culls? It is said that one breeder has used these dogs in his American Bulldog breeding program. Many more exotic breeds are suspected of being crossed into Bulldog lines as well, such as the Dogo Argentino and the Dogue de Bordeaux. Being much more fond of smaller, lighter working dogs than I am of needlessly huge beasts, I suggested to one American Bulldog breeder recently that he cross a good Bulldog to a Rat Terrier/Boston Terrier cross for me, but though he seemed tempted, he never did it, to the best of my knowledge. Who knows what other breeds might have been added to American Bulldog blood recently? We know only that when someone describes his or her American Bulldog as being purebred, with nothing else added to it, either they are thinking very short term or they don't know what they are saying.

So there you have it, the truth, for a switch! In light of this, does it make sense to wonder what the origin, the heritage, of the American Bulldog is? Possibly. After all, whatever has been done to the Bulldog, some have remained about the same from times before any of us were born. But it does not make sense to think of this breed as being purely an expression of the original Elizabethan Bulldogge, transplanted to and preserved in the New World. This, it isn't. Much more important than what the Bulldog was is

Deuce has one imposing mug.

what the Bulldog should be. Fortunately, this is a question we can answer.

I am a firm believer that the American Bulldog, as a breed, has grown in size, and diminished in functional ability, in many instances beyond recognition. Let's remember what this dog was intended to be.

First, it was intended to be a catch dog. Second, it was intended to be a property and livestock protection dog, but its primary usage was catch work, it should never have been a very man-aggressive or even explosively dog-aggressive breed (as such a dog would be useless as a catch dog). Probably, it was a fighting dog. The majority of these dogs in days gone

The author's dog Gumbo, half-American Bulldog and half-Catahoula Leopard Dog, with the author's son Dan. What a watchdog Gumbo was!

by were bred for farm and ranch work first, while a small proportion were used as dog fighters, but this use is definitely part of this breed's history.

Again, as the breed's primary function was undoubtedly catch work early on, early Bulldogs would have to have been primarily interested in catching livestock, rather than fighting hounds, in order to have served their owners well.

A very large dog is useless in catch work. A catch dog should be large enough to get a free-range hog's attention, in no uncertain terms, but should be small and quick enough to move in a manner that will allow it to stay alive while latched to the ear of one of the most dangerous mammals in the

Lyla with Chuck Koura, one of the
author's good buddies. Lyla is out of
Bessie by Bandit.

world. As such, a 70-pound dog is ideal, an 85-pound dog is reaching the upper end of the size limit, and a 100-pound dog is probably too big to catch and hold a real feral hog without being killed.

A very large dog is unnecessary as a manstopper, and a very large Bulldog is unnecessary as a protector of livestock against predators common to the American Southeast. An 85-pound Bulldog is more dog than a human attacker can handle, and I have been told that a man who knows how to handle himself against a dog can literally stay out of the way of a 130-pound Bulldog, rendering it incapable of doing him any damage. (I turned down the chance to view a video tape of a man doing this sent to my house one time.

Drew Koura calls this his Weener Dog, a Rat Terrier—Boston Terrier mix that is a game ratter. The author has seen these Weener Dogs at work—"It isn't pretty."

I don't know what I was thinking.) Meanwhile, your average "wild dog" (feral dog) that would be doing livestock harm wouldn't stand a chance against a good, 80-pound Bulldog. Consider all of this against the backdrop of what a farmer/ rancher is willing to spend on dog food. Why would he own a 130-pound Bulldog when an 80-pounder will do better work for less food?

Finally, American fighting dogs are not very large dogs. American Bulldog fighters of days gone by would have been matching their dogs against Pit Bull Terriers, and pit men back when, as well as today, were not interested in fighting their dogs against a dog three times their dog's weight. A 70-pound Bulldog would have been large for finding a match,

Perdi, owned by Larry Koura. This
bitch is out of Starbuck by Pistol.
Larry admits that he can find some
Catahoula Leopard Dog in Perdi's
pedigree. Such honesty is dreadfully
rare with breeders these days.

while a 130-pound Bulldog would have been perceived as an
absurd match for a Pit Bull.

Big Bulldogs were bred in response to the demands of
novice prospective Bulldog owners. These prospective owners
were not farmers who really needed a working dog. They were
city dwellers, like me, who wanted, and often needed, a dog
that was downright frightening to look at, to scare potentially
dangerous would be intruders away from their homes, their
wives, their children, etc. While a Bulldog of working size
was formidable looking, a huge blob of a monster Bulldog

Hines's old Battle Axe, a 75-pound daughter of Snowbird, one of the most impressive dogs ever known. Snowbird was a hard-hitting hogdog, whose spine-chilling performances Bill captured on video tape. She had zero fear and was the most athletic dog imaginable, and yet just as sweet as can be.

sent a message that was even clearer: "Come into my home, and this dog will kill you!" So this is what they asked for, this is what they paid (anything) for, and this is what, in response to this demand, Bulldog breeders began to produce.

Many city dwellers are beginning to realize that size is not enough to scare off a serious intruder, and if size is what is desired, there are other serious dogs of great size out there to choose from. Just as many a novice Pit Bull owner is beginning to demand more than size, heavy bone, overall bulk, and an awe-inspiring appearance in his dog, hopefully many a novice prospective American Bulldog owner will begin to demand a Bulldog of working size and temperament as well. Just as nature hates a vacuum, supply-and-demand economics hates one even worse, and when

Rode Hawg Bonehead, owned by Larry Koura. Bonehead is out of Bridgette by Zeke.

Rode Hawg Bridgette, owned by Larry Koura.

prospective puppy purchasers begin to demand a real, old-time, functionally capable Bulldog, I think many of us will be surprised at how quickly such dogs will dominate the bloodlines again.

In addition to its being high time that we begin to eliminate oversized, functionally incorrect American Bulldogs from the gene pool, it is also high time for us to eliminate dogs which have been "outcrossed" to other breeds from the gene pool. The easiest way to increase size, decrease size, change the length of muzzle, shorten the back, etc., of one's Bulldogs is to breed in another breed that has the desired characteristics well established in its genetic makeup. But what would we think of a breeder who did this with his Dobermans, for example? Would we respect him? Would we overlook it? We would not. We would think he was a liar and a cheat. So why do we overlook it when a breeder does this with his American Bulldogs? We shouldn't. We should

ZWs Sugar, residing in Germany, is a pretty Bulldog bitch. It's good to see this American breed appreciated outside the U.S., isn't it?!

purchase our puppies only from breeders who have good reputations for breeding nothing but Bulldogs to nothing but Bulldogs, and establishing their lineage the hard way.

Let me leave you with a tip that you might care to use in your next purchase of an American Bulldog. When you've settled on a breeder you respect, ask to see grown pups (or at least pictures of them) from the parents of the pup you are interested in. But do not settle once you've seen one of the grown pups from this breeding. Instead, ask to see all of them. Ask to see an entire litter, or at least for the phone numbers of the owners of each of the dogs from a previous litter, and once you've examined these dogs, ask yourself if, upon maturity, they look like littermates. Will this breeding that you are about to put a deposit on yield dogs of consistent appearance and quality? If not, how can you possibly expect to know what it is that you are about to buy?

It will be interesting to see where the American Bulldog goes from here. The breed has come so far, so quickly, and has been transformed into something it was never intended to be so quickly, that I predict that things can only get better than what they are now. I urge any of you who are in search of an American Bulldog to get past the desire to buy a huge dog, for the sake of size alone. Instead, think about what the history of this breed would have produced had it not been for the recent explosion of interest in Bulldogs by novice puppy buyers. Good pups are still available. Get one from working stock. Support the breeder of working Bulldogs before it's too late.

Mike Harlow's Patch and a zillion puppies. She looks pretty well resigned to her role.

European-bred American Bulldog pups.

Rode Hawg Ully is out of Miss Molly B by Bandit.

Paul Newman was nice enough to share this photograph of himself with his Catahoula Leopard Dog, a breed that is closely associated with the American Bulldog. The author acknowledges Mr. Newman's generosity for this photograph— there's something about a love of dogs that brings people together. The author's wife notes that Mr. Newman would pick a Leopard Dog to own as both he and the Catahoula were known for their stunning blue eyes.

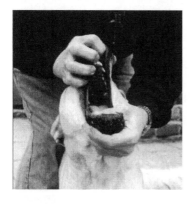

Top left: Hawkens, the American Bulldog sire of the author's dog Gumbo. *Middle left:* Jerry Briffa prying his Cur's "black mouth" open. *Bottom left:* Hawkens. *Top right:* Rose Pitra and Missy, a good-looking hard bitch bred by none other than Sylvester Stallone. Missy's sire was named Stallone. *Bottom right:* Missy with A.J. Pitre, who describes her as loyal to the core, protective, smart, quick and hard as steel.

Top left: Brent Power's Judge, a seven-month-old pup by Bill's Hillbilly. *Bottom left:* Brent Power's Chiquita, a hard little bitch at six months of age. This pretty puppy is out of Country Boy and Snowbird—she's built for work. *Top right:* The author's son Alex with a white Catahoula Bulldog at the home of Gerry Pleasant. Alex wanted to bring the dog home, but didn't. He grew up to weigh over 100 pounds.

Top: Rode Hawg Ully.

Middle: Hines's Debbie Do, a 72-pound daughter of Country Boy out of Dinky Do. This is the ideal-size American Bulldog, the size required before people began to demand huge dogs.

Bottom: Billy Hines's Country Boy, a big dog that can move.

Perdi Cruella, protecting the author's buddy
Drew Koura.

European-bred Bulldog.

Champion Bridgette owned by Larry Koura. She is by Pistol
out of Starbuck.

A good-looking Bandog (Pit Bull to Neapolitan Mastiff cross),residing in Germany, that clearly shows both sides of its heritage. They are not a breed unto themselves, but more of a crossbreed.

BANDOG

Since the publication of my first book, many readers have gotten in touch with me in order to express interest in one of the unusual breeds I wrote about. I guess I can't go so far as to say that more interest has been expressed in the Bandog than any other breed mentioned in *The World of Fighting Dogs*, but I can tell you that, with the possible exception of the American Bulldog, those expressing an interest in the Bandog have been at least as numerous as those expressing an interest in any other breed I discussed. As a result of the interest being expressed in these dogs on the part of dog enthusiasts and prospective dog owners generally, I thought it to be especially surprising that these

Jonathan Shiloka with Bandog visiting
Paris. The author has climbed the Eiffel
Tower many times and enjoyed dinner
at the Restaurant Jules Verne. "Ask for
a window seat!"

dogs almost went out of existence shortly after *The World of Fighting Dogs* was published.

I've given a great deal of thought to what became of the Bandog and why more breeders didn't become involved in producing it. After all, when we first began to hear about these Neapolitan Mastiff, English Mastiff and Pit Bull crosses, dogmen everywhere intuitively knew that when well bred these would simply have to be among the hardest personal protection dogs that the world had ever known. We all knew each of these breeds to be immensely powerful, loyal to their owners to the core, and responsive when given commands. We felt that what was not especially great, from a personal protection point of view, in any one of these breeds, was corrected by breeding it to the others. Sure enough, as puppies began to be born and to mature, they were everything dogmen had expected.

These dogs were almost exclusively an east-coast phenomenon. It was in New York and northern New Jersey that dogmen conceived the idea of creating these dogs, experimented with breeds to be used, and experimented with proportions of Pit Bull, Neapolitan Mastiff, and sometimes English Mastiff and even other breeds, to be used in this crossbred dog. It was also in the Northeast that a few dog fighters began to experiment with Bandogs, and where men interested in protection work first began to use these dogs on other men. When *The World of Fighting Dogs* came out, readers of the book immediately became interested in Bandogs, and these dogs disappeared. Why? What happened?

Having thought this question through, I believe that a few things happened, all of which contributed to the sharp decline in the availability of Bandog puppies. The first, and the most obvious, was the fact that the Neapolitan Mastiff began to grow in popularity at the same time that prospective dog owners began to take an interest in Bandogs. As the most popular means of producing a Bandog was to cross a male Pit Bull Terrier to a Neapolitan Mastiff bitch, the question that the owner of a Neapolitan bitch had to ask himself was one of basic economics. A purebred Neapolitan Mastiff would command fully twice the price, if not more, than a Bandog, for no good reason whatsoever (other than basic supply and demand). This being the case, if a litter of Neapolitan Mastiff puppies was worth twice as many dollars

Jonathan Shiloka's Bandog in Egypt. This darn dog sure
gets around!

to the owner of the bitch being bred as a litter of Bandogs
out of that same bitch, there was absolutely no economic
incentive to breed Bandogs, while the incentive to breed
Neapolitans was great. The breeders did what most of us
would do under similar circumstances: they bred dogs they
could sell at a higher price.

Second, at precisely the same time that the Bandog was
being billed as the answer for those who would love to own
a Pit Bull, but for the fact that the Pit Bull was a smaller
dog than they would prefer to own, many Pit Bull breeders
began to produce larger dogs. Overnight, it seemed, Pit
Bulls became available which could be expected to mature
at almost the size of a Bandog. Those prospective puppy

purchasers who might have looked to the Bandog as a way of owning what they perceived to be a 100-pound, crossbred Pit Bull suddenly had the option of owning what they perceived to be a purebred, 100-pound Pit Bull. This diminished any demand there might have been for the Bandog.

Third, at precisely the same time that the Bandog became known to dogmen outside the inner circle in the Northeast, the American Bulldog became known to dogmen outside the inner circle in the Southeast. Just as the emergence of very large Pit Bulls on the scene had given prospective dog owners less of a reason to buy a Bandog, the appearance of the American Bulldog on the scene gave these same prospective puppy buyers even less reason to obtain a Bandog. (We might include the Tosa here too, as a dog that filled the Bandog niche, but to a much lesser extent than either the oversized Pit Bull or the American Bulldog.) The combination of these three factors gave breeders who might have become interested in producing Bandogs for their own esoteric reasons virtually no economic incentive to do so, and the Bandog faded into nonexistence, for all practical purposes.

None of the experimental lines of Bandogs from the 1970s survives today. This is to say that none of today's Bandogs, to the best of my knowledge, descended from the Bandogs that predated my first book.

The reality is that the only connection to the Bandogs of those days is the name, "Bandog," which originally came from the old English itself, and the general idea that a cross between a Pit Bull and a large, shorthaired Mastiff of one type or another might produce a good, loyal protection dog.

Today, a few breeders worldwide have become interested in producing and in keeping Bandogs. Possibly because in *The*

World of Fighting Dogs, I expressed a preference for specifically the Neapolitan Mastiff to Pit Bull cross, the vast majority of today's Bandogs is produced this way, the modification being that for simple economic reasons, today's Neapolitan to Pit Bull cross is generally the result of a Neapolitan Mastiff dog being crossed to a Pit Bull bitch. The puppies, as it turns out, come out about the same as they did when the sexes were reversed, and the bitch apparently does not suffer excessively during either pregnancy or delivery. It may also be the case that regardless of anything I wrote in my first book, the Neapolitan Mastiff to Pit Bull cross occurs to many a dog enthusiast as being a natural one. Who knows?

Bandog pups from California, the result of a game-bred red-nosed Pit Bull to a female Neo cross.

Bandog with owner Murray Pierce of
Montana. Murray also owns a Tosa.

In any event, I don't know if it makes sense to talk about
Bandogs anymore. I am unaware of anyone who is trying
to perfect these dogs as a pure breed. Furthermore, there
have never been many Bandogs, and there aren't many
people working on producing these dogs today. If we want
to continue to use this term to describe a dog produced by
crossing a Neapolitan Mastiff to a Pit Bull, we can do so.
We could also simply call such a dog a Pit Bull crossed to
a Neapolitan Mastiff, and this way, everybody would know

The Bandog is an extremely loyal and protective of its human family. This particular dog from the Netherlands is a Pit Bull-Neo cross.

exactly what we were talking about. If we are going to use the term to describe the result of a first-or second-generation cross between a Pit Bull and any large, shorthaired Mastiff, I think the term is definitely too vague. It doesn't mean anything specific enough for us to hang our hats on. There are people out there still crossing these dogs in an effort to produce a different kind of protection dog, and as long as the effort is being made, I have no desire to discourage them by counting the Bandog out. Instead, I will leave this subject by saying, very simply, let's see where this kind of dog goes from here.

This is Sammy Holloway with one of his bandogs in the California desert.

Bandogs are hard biters but not good barkers. Sammy Holloway says that the dogs do very well in Schutzhund, but it's hard to make them bark when they should. *Above*: Lucero's Jaws, a 126-pound, 13-month-old, first-generation Bandog. *Below*: Lucero's Sha-Nae-Nae, a 98-pound, 16-month-old, third-generation Bandog.

Above: Jonothan Shiloka playing with his Bandog in the sands of Egypt in front of a pyramid. The author connected Jonothan with the breeder of this Bandog, and he's been in touch frequently (calling from around the world—never collect!). *Bottom left:* Cujo, a half-English Mastiff-half-Pit Bull cross from Perth, Australia, weighs 127 pounds and is an extremely athletic dog. Photograph courtesy of Eddie Smith. *Bottom right:* Bandog produced by crossing of Sharkey, a male Pit Bull, with Ugly, a female Neo. The dog is wet in the photo, courtesy of Sammy Holloway.

Oscar V. Alcaringque of Park Avenue Bordeaux.

DOGUE
de BORDEAUX

Years ago I took a drive with my elder son Alex from our home in New York to Washington, D.C., for an extended weekend. Alex generally accompanies me on virtually every outing I go on. Alex had been wanting to see some of the famous sites in D.C. for a long time, so he had jumped at the opportunity to come with me on this particular trip, even though he understood that the primary reason for the trip was not sightseeing, but rather attending a dog show sponsored by the American Rare Breed Association (ARBA).

I had never gone to the ARBA show before, and I was absolutely fascinated by what I found there on this first trip. In this particular year, the show was held right on the Mall,

The author's buddy, Chief Gerry
Pleasant of the Hartford, Connecticut,
Police Department, on his farm with his
13-month-old Dogue de Bordeaux.

directly in front of the Capitol Building. Many rare breeds were represented by numerous dogs of each breed. Top judges had been flown in from their native lands in order to judge each breed authentically.

As much of a roaring success as this show was, in my eyes, no judging better exemplified, to me, just how far the rare breed scene had come in this country than the judging

The author's friend Juanita Tsai
with her male Bullmastiff Foo
Foo and her female Bordeaux
Dogue Ursula.

of the Bordeaux Dogues did. I was amazed by it. It was as if some very old, very foreign, almost impossible dream of mine had come true.

Not only were numerous Bordeaux Dogues represented, but they were all of high quality. They were spirited dogs as well, and did not come off as the brain-dead specimens that we so often observe at American dog shows. Owners of Bordeaux Dogues had traveled from far and wide to participate in this show, and the judging was conducted by none other than Professor Raymond Triquet himself. Triquet is recognized by French Bordeaux Dogue enthusiasts as being the expert among experts in the breed, and it was clear to me that he took the judging of these dogs at the DC show very seriously. He liked what he saw as he looked these American

Bordeaux Dogues over, and so did I. I was very flattered by the fact that Prof. Triquet greeted me at the show, and that he remembered who I was.

When *The World of Fighting Dogs* was published there were virtually no Bordeaux Dogues in the United States, and worse, there was virtually no interest in this breed among American purebred enthusiasts. At the time, there were at most only 600 Bordeaux Dogues in the world, and very few in Europe outside of France. I wrote the chapter on the Bordeaux Dogue for that first book knowing no one would have any idea what I was talking about and wondering if anyone would care. I wrote an article or two for a widely distributed purebred dog magazine back then too, long before the ads for this breed that are so common now first made their appearance. Back then I would never have believed how far the breed would come in so short a time.

Major efforts were made to bring this breed to the attention of American purebred enthusiasts and before time forgets the names of the people who made the initial efforts, I take this opportunity to mention a few names. First and foremost was Dr. Philip Todd, who once I wrote to regularly and now I haven't chatted with in years. "Doc Todd" was, and I assume still is, a medical doctor with the American military. He had discovered the breed while working in Holland, and he had made early efforts of his own to introduce the breed to the American purebred fancy, but he traveled too much and worked too hard in his career to have the impact that he would have liked to had. When he learned of my interest in the breed, he was as cooperative as any real hobbyist could be, sending me pictures, general information, lengthy letters, and references which got me in touch with important names

Garry Gillard's Vesuvio Le Murdock at eight months of age. The author requested that Garry, a friend from Australia, take a great scenic picture for this book. Here's the fine photograph he sent of his Bordeaux pup. His head is perfect, especially for such a young dog

on the French dog scene. Wherever you are now "Doc Todd," in my estimation you are a large part of the reason the Bordeaux Dogue exists in the United States today.

Another name is, of course, Prof. Raymond Triquet, the French judge who "Doc Todd" first put me in touch with. Triquet took a great deal more time than he had to and extended much effort to see to it that I had appropriate, accurate information about the breed to relay to the American purebred fancy.

There was also Steve and Wendy Norris, who traveled to France, and all over this country, buying dogs from the French and showing them to Americans. They took their breeding seriously, and they sold puppies, when they had pups to sell, responsibly. They viewed this as a sport, rather

Above: The Chateaux Loudenne in the Medoc in Bordeaux, France, the original homeland of the Dogue de Bordeaux. That's the author's sons running on the lawn. This photograph gives us some insight into where the breed came from and what the breed is for. This huge and powerful breed makes sense on these expansive properties in France.
Below: A home in France that the author and his family passed on their way from Bordeaux to Perigord.

The author standing in front of a vineyard in the Medoc of Bordeaux. As you can see, even today there is plenty of room for ownership of a large breed like the Bordeaux Dogue. Visiting this part of Europe puts ownership of these monsters in perspective. Bordeaux Dogues were not bred to live in city apartments.

than a business, and they brought the breed a long way from home in their enthusiasm and with their honesty. It's a shame that this sport and the politics so often alienate people like them, isn't it?

Anyway, for the benefit of anyone who is still unfamiliar with the Bordeaux Dogue, let me describe it as a fine, ancient Mastiff that time has not managed to change. It is a calm, steady dog, but the breed generally has maintained much of its original character. They are a mild-mannered dog, and a trustworthy, steady breed, and highly capable guard dogs can be found among modern Bordeaux Dogue stock. A Bordeaux Dogue in its protective mode is a sight to behold, I can assure you. This is a large, powerful, impressive breed.

It is intended as an estate guardian, rather than as a dog for inside the average suburban home.

These dogs are from the famed wine region in southern France, where large vineyard properties with their accompanying "Chateau" are common, and as one sits at one of these Chateaus, looking across the expanse of property containing row after row of vines, one can just imagine how well suited the Dogue is to this kind of life. Is it any wonder that a lifestyle very much like that enjoyed by the wealthy landowners, in Italy gave rise to the Masttno Napolitano, the Neapolitan Mastiff, in days gone by? These breeds are an incarnation of that which typifies life on the big estates in southern Europe.

I have been to Bordeaux many times, not only to the city of Bordeaux, but to many of the famed Chateaux as well. On a recent trip, I asked many questions about the condition of the Bordeaux Dogue of many people in Bordeaux, and many questions about the Doguin de Bordeaux (pronounced "Doe Gan" de Bordeaux) as well. The Doguin was a smaller variety of Bordeaux Dogue, with males reaching about 80 pounds. Over the years, many have asked me about these dogs, and as I have been extremely curious about them as well, I set out not only to learn as much as I could about their current condition but also to bring one home with me if I could find one. We (my family and I) had even picked a name for the dog. It was to be called "Sylvan" in honor of a nice man I know who lives in the Bordeaux countryside.

Unfortunately, what I managed to learn about the Doguin is that it doesn't exist anymore. I actually spoke with people in Bordeaux, including Sylvan and Prof. Raymond Triquet, who remembered the Doguin de Bordeaux, but while some

A Bordeaux Dogue bred in Germany. Enthusiasts in the US complain that the Europeans concentrate too much on the Dogue's head and not enough on his hips. Say what you will—that's some head.

assured me that the breed no longer exists, others informed me that they knew it well but, come to think of it, they hadn't seen one of these dogs for many years.

No one I spoke with seemed to mind that there was no longer a Doguin de Bordeaux. Sylvan recalled them fondly, but that was all. Triquet went out of his way to assure me that when he had last seen the breed, it was in poor condition, and so we really weren't missing anything by not having any around anymore.

I take a different view of the extinction of the Doguin. Its passing reminds me how veiy close we were to witnessing the passing of many of these rare breeds of antiquity. After all, even the American Bulldog was close to nonexistence

Park Ave Tutt of Norris Place,
Group winner at the Cherryblossom
rare-breed show in
Washington, D.C.

when I met it. The Presa Canario, the Tosa, and other breeds could also have been lost. But interest in these breeds was somehow kept alive and the dogs survive today as a result. Not so for the Doguin de Bordeaux, a breed I bet I would have loved to own. Possibly some day, using Bordeaux Dogue and maybe French Bulldog stock, someone will attempt the reconstruction of the Doguin de Bordeaux. But for now, it is gone, and in its pure form, it is gone forever.

It is tempting to extol the virtues of and to describe the history of the Bordeaux Dogue to you here, yet again, but we have already done this. Suffice it to say that the Bordeaux Dogue is a very large, very powerful animal, and as such, it is certainly not the best choice for a dog to be kept in a small place. In Bordeaux, these are estate guardians and it is on

A litter of Garry Gillard's pups romping around with their mom.

estates such as those in the South of France that the Dogue is most at home. It is a calm and easy to get along with dog, however, and so any large fenced piece of property is a place that this breed can call home.

Generally speaking, this is not an outwardly aggressive breed, though I have seen some Bordeaux Dogues that were very protective of their home. It's a scary sight, by the way, and not one that any intruder in his right mind would ignore. This breed can be dog aggressive too, and I have seen male Bordeaux Dogues that, had they been free to move, would certainly have engaged in combat. But dog aggression in this breed is not as much of a problem as it is among many breeds that we live with today.

This is a "slobbery" dog. Some breeds are worse in this regard, but not much worse. If slobber bothers you, as it does me, then this is not the breed for you. This is also not a long-lived dog. I have heard of Bordeaux Dogues living to be ten,

Oscar of Park Avenue Bordeaux.

or more, years of age, but I have heard of many that have died much younger than this as well. Nonetheless, this is an interesting dog, and if you can live with the above, and if you are inclined to own a big impressive dog, this may well be the breed for you.

In parting, let me repeat that it is good to see the American dog fancy recognizing the Dogue de Bordeaux for what it is. It demonstrates that a serious interest in rare breeds has really taken hold throughout the country and this interest links us ever more closely to purebred dog enthusiasts everywhere. This is an interest that really needs to exist regardless of national boundaries, and these days it certainly does.

Above: A German Dogue
de Bordeaux showing
off his fine head. *Below
left:* Park Avenue Patrick.
Below right: Deng, owned
by Marc Lichtenstein of
Monster Island kennels.

Above left: Deng, owned by Marc Lichtenstein, blasting off! *Above right:* An exhibitor at the ARBA show in Washington, D.C. *Bottom left:* Park Avenue Bordeaux Dogue. *Bottom right:* Tutt of Park Avenue—that's a Bordeaux Dogue!

Above: A line Bordeaux Dogue from Germany. In the right living situation, this is a great breed to own. Wherever you live, you should understand that like many other large mastiffs the Bordeaux is not a long-lived dog.
Below left: Murdock V Alcarinque at home in Holland.
Below right: A fine Bordeaux bitch.

Champion Marcantonio della Nuova Fattoria, a fine Neapolitan
Mastiff from Italy.

NEAPOLITAN
MASTIFF

I must begin this chapter by telling you that the Neapolitan Mastiff is one, big, large, tough, rare, gladiator breed that not only got its start in this country but has come a long way in the United States without any help from me. I remember seeing ads in purebred dog magazines for Neapolitans years ago. True, they were few and far between, but some Italian-Americans brought their bulldogs (and this is what the Italians called these dogs back when) to this country when they first came here.

I have always felt that a good Neapolitan Mastiff, or Mastino Napolitano, is probably the single most impressive animal in all the world of dogdom. Not only the size and the fearsome appearance of these dogs render them awesome

Stoker, a Neapolitan Mastifffrom Canada,
stands 29 inches and weighs 195 pounds.
Stoker is a big fellow.

but also the "presence of mind" of a good Mastino takes me
aback. This breed was once described to me by a famous
Doberman judge as being, in her opinion, the closest thing
to a pure beast among dogs, and she was right. It is a beast.

You should look into buying a Neapolitan Mastiff if
you are interested in owning a dedicated beast, a beast that
will die for you.

Sargent Payne, a six-month-old Neo weighing 95 pounds.
Owner, Dr. Barry Reder.

I sometimes wonder what people think when they read my sometimes very flattering descriptions of a particular breed, go out and buy one, based upon what they think is the research they have done, and ultimately reach a very different conclusion than I did based upon their ownership of a dog that is much less than I described. This can happen, and in the cases of some breeds, it can happen very easily. As time goes on, the chance of getting a really bad Neapolitan Mastiff are reduced, but to reduce them even further, let me tell you what impresses me about what I perceive as being a great Neapolitan Mastiff.

First of all, the Italian breed standard calls for a dog that is smaller than the Neapolitans I have seen that impressed me. I don't know exactly how this came to be the case in Italy, but I think I understand what gave rise to the popularity of smaller Neapolitans (135-pound males) in this country. The dogs I have seen, both in this country and in Italy, were big

Nathan v. Vagentenhof, resting photogenically.

A young Neo advertising for his European breeder. In Italy the breed is known as Mastino Napoletano.

Mastiffs. While bigger is not generally better in the world of purebred dogs, great size is normally preferred among Mastiffs, and while I may prefer smaller Pit Bulls, I prefer larger Mastiffs.

But size is not achieved easily, and this is especially true where very great size is required. Giant dogs often come with more than their fair share of structural problems, and the structural problem that most often afflicted the larger Neapolitan Mastiffs in this country was hip dysplasia. The larger the dog, and the more "typy" the dog, the more likely it was to be dysplastic. The easiest method of dealing with the problem of dysplasia among American Neapolitans was to reduce the size of the dogs selected for, and with the Italian breed standard working in favor of those who would drop

Demon of Dogstar showing off his
leonine profile.

the size rather than dealing with the problem head on, this
is what breeders did.

The structural quality of the dogs being shown improved
dramatically. But while the structural problems were largely
erased, the memories of the rare, but incredible, massive
Neapolitan that did not demonstrate structural problems
were not. I would watch smaller Neapolitans being shown,
and the first thing that would come to mind would be, "Hey!
The dog can move!" The very next thing that would come
to mind would be, "Man, I wonder what ever happened
to those 200-pound plus, square, thick, structurally sound
Neapolitans like the occasional dog I would bang into way
back either here or in Italy?" Those were some impressive
dogs, my friend, and we should not forget them or we will
never know what a truly impressive dog is.

These days, it seems that many Neapolitan Mastiff breeders understand that structural inadequacy is unacceptable, and they are breeding to keep this inadequacy out of their lines. But for the first time, in a long time, the desire to breed Neapolitans that are not structurally faulty, and that display the impressive size of a true Mastiff at the same time is apparently alive again. Personally, I hope this becomes a trend among those who take upon themselves the responsibility of maintaining this breed, because once you lay your eyes upon this large, sound, thick, square, steady, 200-pound plus Neapolitan Mastiff, you will know that this is the dog the breed was intended to be.

The Neapolitan Mastiff is much more than an impressive "looker," however. While there is no doubt that anyone will stand in awe of these dogs because of the incredible appearance of a "good" male alone, one will also quickly come to realize that this is an alert, courageous, very devoted companion dog and guardian. A good Neapolitan will protect you and your property with the best of the guardian breeds in addition to offering a deterrent that is so great as to be almost absurd.

Furthermore, as the owner of one of these dogs, if you have brought it home for the right reason, which is to say if you have brought it home not because you wanted to scare your neighbors and any potential intruder, but because you really wanted to have a companion dog, you will undoubtedly really come to love this dog. It will bond with you. It will love you back. It will reward you if you are good to it. It will become your friend. That, in itself, is worth a great deal to me.

The author received this old photograph from old friend Tony
Jacovine. Pictured is Tony's grandfather's partner Luigi Puca
in front of their store at 131 Mott Street in New York City
between 1927 and 1929. The dog's name can only be properly
pronounced if you speak Neapolitan dialect, but it sounds like
Turto Wallo (and means "All Drool").

Having said all of this, let me tell you that after the publication of *The World of Fighting Dogs*, I got calls from Neapolitan breeders who expressed the concern that I had put people off to the idea of buying a Neapolitan because I talked about how difficult these dogs can be to live with because they drool excessively. I suppose, that I could tell you that the suitability of these dogs as pets depends entirely upon you and how you want to live. I love these dogs, but I wouldn't buy one to keep in my house. They slobber! Often, they smell bad. If this doesn't bother you, then the Neapolitan may be a suitable house dog for you. It is not a suitable house dog for me, and my wife would lose her mind if I were to bring one home. In my estimation, this is a dog for a large piece of property, and if I had that large piece of property, I would want a Neapolitan Mastiff very much. Unfortunately, my property measures 60' by 100', fenced yard included, and this is insufficient space for this kind of dog if you like to live in a clean and orderly fashion.

The Neapolitan Mastiff is a dog with a tremendous history behind it, and as I have talked about this history elsewhere, I will not repeat it here. I will tell you that the very appearance of the dog conveys this ancient history. This is a Mastiff from days gone by, maybe even more so than the Bordeaux Dogue. It is the dog that was produced to guard the property of kings and land barons when the land required to maintain these dogs was available and when the need for this kind of serious protection was great. If for no other reason, this is a dog that should survive, in as pure a form as possible, forever.

Nerone as a puppy, photographed in Italy.

Litterbox full of German-bred Neo puppies.

European-bred Neapolitan Mastiff.

Left: Deer Run Rufus,bred by Tobin Jackson and owned by Joseph and Debbie Mullusky. *Right:* Champion Blacho-O Ruga at six months of age, bred and owned by Joseph and Debbie Mullusky.

Left: Carlotta of Dogstar kennels wearing her Italian collar. *Right:* A young puppy, not yet cropped.

Right: Danny, a former Israeli Special Forces soldier, with one of his male Neos. Having once bred in Israel, Danny and his wife now breed Neos in New York City, where they provide more than ample security! *Below*: The impressive Cesare of Somerwood at eight months of age, sired by Italian Champion Hatrim out of Ruga. Owners, Joseph and Debbie Mullusky.

Above left: A not very good picture of a very good Neo, Paestor of the Thatched Roof, weighing 165 pounds (the author's guess confirmed by the owner). *Above right*: Paestor at the FCI show in Eindhoven, Holland, in February 1997. *Below*: Vittoria Del Nolano at 15 months of age, owned by Sig. M. De Falco of Del Nolano kennels in Italy.

Above: Sheba of Dogstar. *Below left:* Jeyna Adereth behind her Neo. *Below right:* A good Neo at the Holland FCI show, photographed by the author. It's helpful to keep an eye on what's going on around the world to be sure you still know what a good dog looks like.

David Leavitt, founder of the Olde English Bulldogge breed, with one of his pups. Dave worked on this breed for many years, finally perfecting a dog that breeds true, worthy of the attention of bulldog enthusiasts everywhere. His project has taken on a life of its own. There's much to be said for that.

OLDE ENGLISH
BULLDOGGE

It was in 1971 that Dave Leavitt, then of Spring Grove, Pennsylvania, began the breeding project that was to give rise to a reconstruction of the Bulldogs of Elizabethan England, called by Leavitt the Olde English Bulldogge. In my first book *The World of Fighting Dogs*, I told you that Leavitt is a former Bulldog (show variety) enthusiast who became disenchanted with that breed due to the utter lack of physical ability it demonstrated and the health problems that are so common to it. He set to work on a breeding project that he felt would produce Bulldogs that were more physically fit, in all respects, and so would be better representatives of the Bulldogs or "Bulldogges of Olde." Hence, the current existence of the Olde Bulldogge.

Before going on here, let's begin our discussion of these dogs with a few words on the pronunciation of the breed name. Over the years I have heard the name of the Olde Bulldogge pronounced "Oldee Bulldoggy," "Old Bulldoggy" and "Oldee Bulldog." The proper pronunciation of the breed name is simply "Old Bulldog." The spelling comes from the Middle English.

On the one hand, I have felt for a long time that Leavitt's pursuit was a noble one, and that a recreation of a good, healthy, athletic Bulldog, like the one's there used to be, was a great idea. From this perspective, it doesn't surprise me in the least to see that all these years later there is still great interest in the Olde Bulldogge. On the other hand, this has been so much a one-man project, even where others have become involved in it, that it's amazing, really that it should still be alive and strong in the 21st century. After all, Leavitt came up with this idea by himself. He began the breeding project that was to give rise to a "breed" all alone. He sold his pups to those he could trust to take good care of the dogs, and to those who had an interest in his "mission," and he kept careful records of what was going on. After all these years, when you speak with Dave today, he can "talk dogs" with the best of them. It all goes to demonstrate a tremendous commitment. After all, how many breeders are you aware of who have been this involved in any breed for this length of time.

But time has taken its toll on Dave, and while he is as knowledgeable a dogman as he ever was, and while he is as interested as he has ever been in his Olde Bulldogges, he is not as involved in the breeding of his dogs as he once was. In fact, as of today, while Dave still keeps many dogs (I think I

Bongo, a smiling adult male Olde
English Bulldogge.

counted seven or nine that he made reference to as we spoke
recently) only one of his dogs is an Olde Bulldogge, and this
is a stud that he keeps for breeding to select females. Most
of the dogs Dave has around today are "rescue dogs," or dogs
that he has taken from some shelter before their time came
to be put down, and it is primarily to such rescue work that
Dave is now devoted.

Dave didn't get tired of his dogs, or of the breeding of his
dogs, as near as I can tell, but rather, like so many a dogman
I have known, he got tired of the people that the dogs
brought him into contact with. He got tired of responding to
numerous inquiries from those who would reserve puppies
from an upcoming breeding, only to have no interest in
buying a dog when the litter was finally ready to go. He got
tired of trying to find suitable homes for the pups he had

Dave Leavitt in front of his kennels in Pennsylvania.

devoted so much time and effort to bringing into this world. So now he is content to allow others to do his breeding and to deal with the headaches associated with breeding dogs, while he stays on top of what an Olde Bulldogge is supposed to be and while he keeps people on the same track that he defined with his years of work and dedication.

As you can imagine, this plan of Dave's has given rise to a few major problems. After all, when you have sold puppies to people who have, in turn, dedicated themselves to the breed, it is to be expected that these people will eventually conceive a few ideas of their own with regard to the specific direction the breed should take. In some instances, differences of opinion may not take the grand form of "Officially Changing Direction," but rather a difference of opinion may arise over the question of exactly what dog a particular bitch should be bred to in one particular instance. For example, a particular breeder of Olde Bulldogges may feel that it is time to breed

Polly, Dave Leavitt's foundation bitch, not only was good looking, athletic, high spirited, and trainable, she lived to be 18 years old! Furthermore, one of Polly's daughters (whom Dr. Semencic knew) also lived to be 18. Both bitches were active and well until the day she died.

to a particular stud because the line of dogs he or she is working with now requires more mass, while Dave feels that considerations such as this one should always be secondary to the matter of athletic ability. Who wins an argument like this one?

You may think this is an easy question to answer. After all, if I buy a purebred Doberman bitch, and I decide the line of dogs I will produce requires more size, I am free to breed the bitch I paid for to whoever is willing to breed his dog to my bitch, right? Right. But in this case, we aren't talking about Dobermans. In fact, we are talking about a unique situation in the world of dogs, as far as I am concerned. We are dealing with a breed of dog developed by one man who

Besse, an adult female Olde English Bulldogge.

is still alive and who is still actively involved in establishing the direction of the breed. As Dave said when I spoke with him the other day, 'This is not a Democracy!" I couldn't have said it better myself.

These are Dave's Bulldogges and while Dave is here to tell us what a Dave Bulldogge should be, there is no question as to, or debate about, what a Bulldogge should be. I must tell you that years ago, and even now, when I slip and forget that people often don't know what I am talking about when I refer to the breed as "Dave Dogs." From my point of view, Dave can only be right when he says that the breeding of these dogs is not based upon anyone's opinion but his own. I think that anyone who wants to take a new direction in the breeding of Olde Bulldogges should first think of a suitable breed name because the product of any breeding which does not meet with Dave's approval can never be a "Dave Dog."

316

Mike Walz's first litter of pups out of Rosa by Zeke.

In any event, I am sure you can see how it came to pass that trouble cropped up in this breed in the past. To avoid such trouble, before buying an Olde Bulldogge, I suggest that you ask Dave what he thinks about a prospective purchase. If you can track him down, he'll undoubtedly be happy to tell you, but I wouldn't bother him until the night before you are ready to pick up your puppy as he sounds like he has about had it with those who talk but who have no real interest. If you can't track him down and please don't ask me to do it for you, ask the person you are buying the pup from for a way to get in touch with Dave. Buy your pup from a "Dave Approved" breeder.

In order to help prospective Olde Bulldogge puppy purchasers secure a pup that Dave Leavitt considers to be well bred, in all respects, he has set forth the following

A sturdy, well-put-together male
puppy.

requirements for the Olde English Bulldogge Association
(OEBA).

APPROVED BREEDER REQUIREMENTS

Approved breeder status is bestowed by the OEBA on
those breeders who are establishing breeding schemes under
OEBA direction.

Approved breeders must adhere to the OEBA Approved
Breeder Requirements and the OEBA Breeding Stock
Selection Requirements. Approved breeders must clearly tell
dog buyers that only the best examples of the breed will be
issued Certificates of Merit, which will allow breeding.

Approved breeders must be ethical in all dog transactions.
All dogs must be sold with a guarantee of replacement if

Eight-day-old puppies—handle with care.

subsequent lameness, disability, or death is due to genetic causes.

Approved breeders will provide the following minimum care to dogs housed outside. Runs will be at least 48-square feet, with shading supplied during the summer. Shelter will be constructed in such a manner that the dog will stay warm in the winter. Adequate food of a good quality will be provided. Fresh water must be available at all times. Manure will be cleaned up at least once a day.

Approved breeders must tend to the bitch during whelping. It is helpful to break the sack, cut the umbilical cord, dry the pup with a towel and place it on a nipple. If uterine inertia develops, a black discharge is observed or labor continues for more than two hours with no delivery, then veterinary help must be summoned immediately. Pups must be checked for cleft palates as soon as possible. Pups

Left: Zeke is a five-year-old male, the foundation stud of Mike Walz's breeding program. *Right:* Flash, at seven months of age, cooling off.

possessing such a defect should be culled promptly, as they would slowly die otherwise.

Approved breeders will place the bitch in her whelping box no later than 50 days after the first mating, in order that she become acclimated. Heat will be provided to keep the boxes at least 80 degrees F., until the pups are a minimum of 18 days old. Dogs and people must be kept away from the box to protect against fights, disease, and nervousness.

Approved breeders must register their litters with the OEBA no later than one month after their birth. The litter must be inspected by the OEBA President. If necessary, the inspection can be accomplished by the breeder sending the OEBA a video tape which shows the pups, one at a time. All four sides should be shown and the tails must be clearly displayed. The breeder will submit the date of birth,

Certificate of Merit numbers of Dam and Sire, a list of the pups detailing their sex, color and whether the pup's tail is straight, crooked, or screw.

The OEBA will issue puppy papers to the breeder. Pup buyers will be given these papers, which they should fill out and return to the OEBA along with a fee to receive OEBA registration papers.

Present Evaluators:

David Leavitt

As you can see, Dave isn't kidding.

But enough of the politics of dogs. It seems that every breed is steeped in some absurd, political quagmire and that more time is wasted talking about who dislikes whom than is spent on talking dogs and by so doing, not allowing a breed to advance in quality. I'm sure that you are aware of these politics and that you are tired of them. As you can imagine, I am completely sick of them, and they have turned many good, enthusiastic, honest dog breeders away from dogs all together. As embroiled in politics as Dave undoubtedly is, there is probably less trouble, on a per capita basis, within this breed than among other breeds, so let's not talk about them anymore.

For awhile it seemed that the Olde Bulldogge, as a breed, was going in a direction that was prioritizing docility around people at the expense of "working ability." I began to see the occasional dog that didn't look as if it had the physical ability that I knew to be a priority for Dave in the old days. A few even looked as if they were beginning to approximate the appearance of some of the Bulldogs of the modern show ring, and this, of course, caused me to wonder what the point of the breed was to be, given that it had been established purely

Rosa, owned by Michael and
Marianne Walz, at five years of
age, weighing 55 pounds.

to get away from what the show ring had created. But these days, Dave has entrusted his breeding to a man by the name of Mike Walz, who is very concerned with performance and the maintenance of physical ability.

Mike's concern for performance, combined with Dave's insistence that no one but an attacker should ever be hurt by a dog that he is in any way responsible for (and Dave's interest in performance as well, mind you), has kept the Bulldogge just about exactly on track, in my opinion. In fact, some time ago, I came across an Olde Bulldogge walking with its owner at a rare-breed show. I don't think the dog was entered, but that it and its owner came as spectators. I told him I thought his dog was a really good one. It wasn't very large (I have never been a fan of unnecessarily large dogs), and it gave a very athletic appearance. It was well built, in all respects, and it could move like a Pit Bull. Those of you who

Resting in the shade is this handsome male
owned by Ray Miller.

are familiar with the show-variety Bulldog will understand
that this is saying quite a bit about a Bulldog of any kind. I
think the fellow who owned the dog felt better when hearing
that I disagreed with his dog's critic. I hope so.

In any event, not very long ago I heard through the
grapevine that Mike Walz had plans to breed one of his
bitches and that he expected the pups to be good, sound,
athletic dogs. To make a long story short, I made a few
inquiries about what dog the bitch was due to be bred to
and, lo and behold, Mike had found the same dog that I
had admired at the rare-breed show and had made plans to
breed to it. From my perspective, this indicates that a positive
direction is being followed even today where the production
of these dogs is concerned.

On occasion I will get calls from young men, just
beginning their families, in search of a dog suited for children.
On the one hand, they want a dog they feel will be safe for
use as a family dog as they will soon have newborn children
in the house. On the other hand, they often approach me

Michael Walz and Zach, a pup out
of Rosa and Zeke.

with some pretty lofty ideas about what they have picked as the ideal dog for them. Only this morning, in fact, I got a call from a young guy whose wife is expecting their first-born child in two months. He had decided that it would be a good idea to have a family dog, as long as he was going to be the head of a family, so he was seriously considering adopting a grown, game-bred male Pit Bull from some virtually unknown source in one month. He asked me if I thought this was a good idea.

Needless to say, I advised against this course of action on his part, but sensing the disappointment in his voice, and knowing that he wanted a dog like this very much, my advice to him was to consider getting an Olde Bulldogge pup. These dogs are known to be exceptional around children. Securing

A tuckered-out male bred by
Dave Leavitt and owned by Julie
Singleton.

a breed with a good reputation around children should
never relinquish a parent of his responsibility to supervise
all activities between a dog and a child, but some choices are
better than others, and the Olde Bulldogge is a good choice.

This is also a breed that has a good record for longevity.
Not only is this saying a great deal in view of the fact that the
modern show-variety Bulldog has the opposite reputation
(and for good reason), but I have read accounts which
suggested that even the Bulldogge of Elizabethan England
tended to be a short-lived dog. While it would be highly
unfair to lead you to expect this kind of longevity from an
Olde Bulldogge, or from any dog, for that matter, I will tell
you that I have known of more than one Olde Bulldogge that
has lived for 18 years and these have stayed in remarkably

Gerry Pleasant with his Olde Bulldogge bitch pup at 11 weeks old. Breeder, Deb Keller.

good condition until the end! One of these was Polly, Dave's foundation bitch. Another was Flash, a daughter of Polly and owned by Don Fiorino and his former wife Sue (a good friend of my wife).

I have also seen really athletic Olde Bulldogges, and I don't simply mean that these dogs looked athletic. Once I was at Dave's house when he lived in Spring Grove, Pennsylvania, and a guy who owned a large, bully, 80-pound-plus male came to visit with his dog. For fun, Dave hung a spring pole on a tree and the dog immediately jumped up and grabbed it. We watched the dog bounce up and down from the tree for awhile, and finally Dave went into the house and came out with lunch. We all sat down on the grass and ate and talked while the dog continued to bounce up into the tree and back down again, then back into the tree and then back down again. Finally, we finished lunch, took the dog off the spring pole and put the contraption away, but by that time this dog had been on that spring, by choice, for what had to have been at least half an hour if not 45 minutes. Upon being removed from the spring pole, the dog settled down by his master's side and relaxed.

I like these dogs, and I would like to see them become more popular. I'm not sure how this can be achieved, though, as the dog is maintained best when Dave stays personally involved in its breeding. Maybe this is not a breed that is ever to become big, and maybe this is a good thing. Maybe some ventures are best kept small and maintained by a select few.

Deb Keller with Champion CoM Valley View's Otis, CGC participating in a rare breed show. The CGC suffix indicates that Otis has passed the American Kennel Club's Canine Good Citizen test.

Manuel Curto's Tomas de Irema Curto. The author relays that while visiting Manuel's kennel, Manuel would not allow him to take photographs (for fear that the photographs would not do his dogs justice). He did present each dog to Dr. Semencic as well as provide a color picture.

CANARY DOG
(EL PERRO DE PRESA CANARIO)

I'll tell you something about writing a book like this one. One doesn't write a book like this from beginning to end. One writes a chapter as the spirit to contemplate the content of a particular chapter moves him, regardless of what place the chapter will occupy in the finished book. I think I know now what form this book will be in when you see it and exactly where this chapter will fit into the finished product, but for your information, regardless of what you may see when you look at the book, this is the last chapter I wrote.

There is a reason for this. The reason is that although I have told you that this book is intended as an update, I have wanted it to be more than an update, but I also wanted it to offer information that was very much "first hand," as opposed to the kind of regurgitated stuff we so often see in dog books.

I think *The World of Fighting Dogs* was a somewhat different kind of dog book for a couple of reasons. For one thing, it defined a category of dogs that had not previously been defined, i.e., the fighting dogs. For another thing, it wasn't as if I could have read somebody else's book or somebody else's article about the Bandog, or the American Bulldogs, or the Olde Bulldogge, etc., and used that information to write my book. There was no information. I made the information by going to the sources myself, either in person, by phone, or in letters, and then I offered a compilation of it in my book, along with my own ideas about what all the information meant.

When I decided to write this book, it is true that I wanted it to be an update. But I also wanted it to be the kind of dog book that I think *The World of Fighting Dogs* was and is. I wanted this book to offer you information that was accurate and unavailable anywhere else, so I made up my mind to collect information for us, for myself and for you, the way I did during the late 1970s and the early 1980s. To this end, last year I gathered up my family and made a trip to Bordeaux, France. I was determined to find something that all but a few Frenchmen would be unaware of the existence of and to bring it back from the brink of extinction. I was determined to find the last of the Doguin de Bordeaux dogs. Unfortunately, after having made the trip and after having talked to the people, what I learned was that I had missed the Doguin by a few years. They were already extinct, by a matter of only a few years.

The author with his sons Alex and Dan on one of
the black-sand beaches of Tenerife.

I made a great contact who has provided me with
information about the Korean Jindo dog, a breed I have been
very interested in for a long time, and a breed that I have
previously been unsuccessful in gathering information about.
I think that bringing my newfound information about the
Jindo Dog to this book is a contribution, but it came to me
too easily, when it finally came. I was looking for something
a little more difficult to secure, so here's what I've done.

I brought my family to the Canary Islands in search of
the finest Canary Dogs (El Perro de Presa Canario) on earth.
I had not found the information necessary to present these
fine dogs to you in time to use it in my first book. I did do an
article or two on the breed after the first book came out, and
I did include a chapter on these dogs in my second book *Pit*

Bulls and Tenacious Guard Dogs. But the information offered in that second book had come from sources in Spain via the mail. Granted, there was a great deal of information, and some very good photographs, all of which I am very grateful for. I had seen Canary Dogs outside of Spain, but it bothered me a little that I didn't know the dogs first hand. I had never seen them in their native environment. So I decided that it would be an interesting adventure to travel to the Canary Islands to correct this shortcoming on my part and use the information gathered during the adventure in this book. Bear with me if this chapter gets a bit "traveloguey." I enjoyed this trip, and so did my family, so perhaps you will enjoy hearing a brief description of the relevant parts of it.

The Canary Islands are owned by Spain, but they are situated much further from Spain than they are from North Africa. In fact, they lie between 80 and 200 miles from the Sahara Desert, while they are roughly 800 miles from mainland Spain. The island of Tenerife, one of seven of the Canary Islands (there are 12 islands, but only 7 are large enough to be counted), is known as a great vacation place for Europeans, especially Germans, the English, and a number of Italians, but they are not well known to American tourists at all. For Americans, the islands are an unlikely place to be.

I am certain that I never would have found myself in the Canary Islands had it not been for my interest in the dogs that are found there, and it is doubtful that I would have made this particular trip had it not been for my activity on the Internet. On the "net" I got into a conversation (via e-mail) with a Spanish purebred enthusiast by the name of Angel Camacho. Angel is a knowledgeable dog person and he is interested in a wide variety of breeds, particularly Spanish

Alex and Dan Semencic in front of the famous
volcano Mt. Tiede, the highest point in all of
Spain, bifurcating the island ofTenerife.

breeds. When I began to question him in depth about Presa
Canario, rather than offer unhelpful answers to my detailed
questions, he put me on the track that lead to experts.

First he led me to the President of the Presa Canario
Club of Tenerife. I wrote to this person and got no answer.
Next, Angel lead me to the President to the Canary Dog
Club of Gran Canaria (another of the islands). I wrote to
this man too, and again I got no answer. I am sure that my
failure to get a response from either of these guys was my
fault, as I wrote them in English, having believed what I had
heard about how widely spoken the English language is in
the Canary Islands. It isn't.

This impressive dog was spotted by the author at Restaurant Otelo in Adejo. Its proud owner told Dr. Semencic that the dog was a 50/50 cross of Canary Dog and Bardino and that he was not dangerous and loved children.

When I questioned Angel further, he told me about the author of a book on Presa Canario, a famous breeder of these dogs who is known throughout Spain as being the expert's expert on the breed. I told Angel that I would write him next, but instead of risking another failure on my part, Angel offered to phone him from the mainland himself and to explain what I was after. He asked me what it was I wanted to ask this man specifically, and after having thought about the answer to that question for a couple of days, I e-mailed Angel back asking him if he'd mind if I dropped by his kennel to talk dogs one day soon.

Camacho explained that this breeder lived in Tenerife, but way on the north side of the island. Furthermore, he said, he lived in an out of the way inland town, at the base of a huge volcano that marks the highest point in all of Spain. He said that getting there would be difficult.

Left: The author with Manuel Curto, photographed by the author's wife Barbara, just outside Manuel's kennels in Tenerife. *Right:* Mory de Irema Curtoisa very impressive Canary Dog bitch. Some argue that these dogs simply look like Pit Bulls. Not so—the coat is entirely different both in color and texture, as is the structure of the dog. The Canary Dog is a breed unto itself and should be appreciated as such.

Now, I've been around. Not only am I not afraid to travel, but I enjoy getting away to less traveled places, and a visit to the Canary Islands sounded like anything but a hardship, so I told Angel to go ahead and ask the guy if he'd mind if I dropped by and spent a day with him. Two days later I had an e-mail in my box telling me that the guy would be happy to chat dogs with the curious American and that I should let him know how soon I could be there.

335

The author's son Alex some years ago
with a Canary Dog owned by Tobin
Jackson, probably imported from South
America. The author doesn't usually like
his kids to get too close to big strange
dogs, but this dog was so steady, he
made an exception.

In no time flat I was on the phone with travel agents and
rummaging through the Sunday paper's travel ads. I quickly
learned that, while a visit to the Canary Islands wasn't as
expensive as I had feared, staying for a week was much
cheaper than staying for a few days and that every price
offered was based on double occupancy. As such, the cost of
taking a second person along was not double the cost of
going alone. This being the case, I figured my wife, Barbara
and I were both going to the Canary Islands and as we didn't
want to go away without the boys, Alex and Dan, I booked
a trip for the four of us. (Think of this story the next time

Isora de Irema Curto, a lighter shaded bridle Canary Dog and a good-looking animal.

someone suggests that you can make big money writing dog books!)

As soon as I had my dates confirmed, I wrote the man in the Canary Islands, Manuel Curto Gracia, and told him that I was on my way. I told him I'd call him the following Monday from my hotel in Playas de las Americas, way on the South side (the wrong side from the perspective of a visitor to Manuel's kennels) of the island of Tenerife, and off we flew.

Dropping down out of the sky onto the Canary Islands is much like touching down on the surface of the moon. The landscape on many parts of the islands is quite lunar, such as the landscapes one will find on the south side of Tenerife, much of the volcano "Tiede," all of Lanzeroti, etc. How do

Nifa de Irema Curto was difficult for the author to assess due to her obvious state of lactation. She is one of Manuel Curto's brood bitches.

I know about lunar landscapes? Have I been to the moon in order to offer this comparison with such authority? No, but the astronaut Neil Armstrong has, and he has also been to Tenerife. According to the tour guide who brought us to the top of the volcano one day, Mr. Armstrong saw a strong comparison between the moon and parts of the Canary Islands. Besides, I have seen pictures of the surface of the moon. I was watching my television carefully when man first set foot on the moon, and the Canary Islands offer some very lunar scenes, I can assure you.

The time difference between New York City and the Canary Islands is only five hours. It's five hours later on the islands than it is in New York. The flights to Tenerife leave in the early evening, so with the time difference factored in, one lands in Tenerife at about 5 AM their time. So you are

Bary de Irema Curto, after just having her pups.
Owner, Manuel Curto.

tired when you get there, and it's dark, but not so dark that you can't see that you've come to one very different kind of place. We made our way through customs, boarded a bus, and after a ride that lasted about a half of an hour, we were at our hotel.

We rested awhile, enjoyed the day, and the following day I phoned Manuel Curto, with the assistance of the hotel's concierge. The first time we called him he asked us to call back in ten minutes because he couldn't hear us for the sound of all the dogs barking on his end. I knew I had the right number, anyway. We called back. It was quieter the second time. I made an appointment to visit with him on Tuesday, as this was the only day that he could have a translator on hand. (It turned out that I amazed myself by remembering much more Spanish than I would have thought possible, but the translator was a great help anyway because Manuel couldn't understand any of my English and there were parts of what he was saying that I couldn't catch either.)

On Monday evening I rented a car and Tuesday morning, bright and early, Barbara, Alex, Dan and I began our drive to the north side of the island. Should anyone plan a drive like this in the future, I advise you to bring a detailed map of Tenerife with you as the maps that we managed to secure there were largely inaccurate. The map defined roads that didn't exist and unfortunately, every one of these nonexistent roads was a direct one to La Esperanza, the town we were in search of. But the island is not a large one, after all, and one really can't get very lost on a "not too large island," so we eventually ended up in town, at the gas station that was to be our meeting point. I called Manuel and the translator he had on hand advised me to sit tight as they would be there to collect us shortly.

I must tell you that at this point I was more than a bit disappointed at the paucity of Canary Dogs to be seen on the island. It seemed that every time I heard a deep bark and turned my head in the direction of it, expecting to get my first glimpse of a Canary Dog in its homeland, I would find myself face to face with a German Shepherd, or some other mainland breed, instead (but specially the German Shepherd). What immediately leapt to mind was the fact that I had written in book two that during the early 1950s, the Presa Canario had almost gone extinct due to the boom in popularity of the German Shepherd on the islands. I guess what I wrote was true: German Shepherds are certainly popular throughout the islands, and they are German Shepherds of good quality.

Guama de Irema Curto, a fine young bitch from Manuel Curto's kennel.

The closer we got to the area of La Laguna, Taco, La Esperanza, etc., the more often I would see mutts of the brindle color that I expected to see on the Presa Canario. We were early getting to La Esperanza, so we stopped in a little cafe for sodas and there was a rich brindle coated mutt sitting in the parking lot. When I asked the owner if he had any Presa Canario in him, the owner remarked that the dog was part Canary Dog. When I asked if it had some German Shepherd in it too, the owner again remarked that the mutt was mostly Presa Canario crossed to German Shepherd, but that it had some other stuff in there too.

Barbara saw the first Presa Canario of the trip. It was in the yard of a private home, and the home was on a narrow road, so there was nowhere to stop unless I pulled into the driveway of the house. With the dog on the loose and my

Left: Tamay de Irema Curto, a good solid bitch with a very typical head. *Right:* Leona de Irema Curto, a very good Canary Dog in the fawn coat color. Although the fawns are not discriminated against, the author is not a fan of this coat color in Canary Dog.

Spanish not good enough to depend upon communicating to the owner what I was doing paying him a visit, I decided to pass it by without a look or a picture, knowing that I would be seeing more Canary Dogs soon.

Finally, we met Manuel Curto and the translator and they took us to the breeding facility. Manuel got out of his Jeep to open the gate and we followed him onto his property. When I stepped out of my rented car, I was immediately greeted, or more appropriately I was sized up by Tomas, a large, structurally perfect (in my less than expert opinion), brindle-coated Canary Dog, and Manuel Curto's primary stud dog. This is what I had traveled so far to see and I was quite enthusiastic about seeing it. Unfortunately, Tomas was somewhat less enthusiastic about meeting me, so Manuel put him on a leash and chained him to a fence post. So restrained, Tomas became a little indignant and focused his

Tsara, a fawn American Staffordshire Terrier, owned by Jan Bracke of Belgium, with some of his Canary Dogs. Jan has four Canary Dogs and one Am Staff—guess which dog he likes best!

indignation upon me, so it quickly became clear to me that Tomas and I would not become the best of friends in the time I had available on this trip.

Manuel showed us into his office where he directed us to sit. He began the conversation by asking the translator to ask me exactly what it was I wanted to know about the Canary Dog. His answer to my first question, and my many questions after that, were all composed and delivered in a professorial manner. This fellow is serious about his dogs and about dog history generally. The following comes largely from my discussion with Manuel Curto Gracia in the office of his kennels on the north side of Tenerife, in the town of La Esperanza, that day. It also comes from past research and from information gathered elsewhere in the Canary Islands on this trip.

In the Canary Dog chapter of my second book I told you that the Canary Islands were actually originally named

Rani, a ten-month-old Canary bitch
owned by Jan Bracke. She stands 19
inches and weighs 93 pounds, but
unfortunately suffers badly from hip
dysplasia.

for the dogs that had been found there by the Spanish
Conquistadors. While this is the commonly accepted theory,
there is apparently a second theory that has a following
on the islands. This theory proposes that the islands were
originally named for a flower found there, and in North
Africa: the Canis flower. Be this as it may, it is misleading to
say that the Canary Islands were named for the Canary Dog
that we know today. In fact, the abundance of dogs found on
the islands when the Conquistadors first arrived there were
smaller dogs.

I said in my last book that the Canary Dog was originally
produced by the crossing of Mastiffs and Bulldogs, brought

Sigi Aler's Canary bitch, named Jessy.

Neron, a three-year-old male Canary Dog owned by Jan Bracke, stands 20.5 inches and weighs about 84 pounds. Jan, who imported this dog from Tenerife, is very honest about his dogs and likes this dog although he is well below the standard in size.

to the islands by English settlers during the 19th century, to the native Canary Island dogs. After having visited the Canary Islands, having chatted with Manuel, having observed the kinds of dogs commonly found there, and having spoken with a few Canary Islanders about their crossbred dogs, I now feel that the above bit of information is overly simplistic. The Canary Dogs are not simply English breeds crossed to native Canary Island breeds at all. In fact, even the dogs from Tenerife are not of exactly the same genetic background as the dogs from Gran Canaria are. The blend of breeds used to perfect the Canary Dogs of Tenerife is a little different than the blend of breeds used to perfect the Canary Dogs of Gran Canaria. This is not to say that dogs from Gran Canaria are not very similar to, and even bred to, dogs of Tenerife. They are. In fact, while I was at Manuel's kennel, one of the

This Canary Dog bitch sports a coat color that is acceptable in the Canary Islands, though she is owned by Show Stopper kennels in the US. At 22 months, she stands 25.5 inches and weighs 117 pounds.

bitches being kenneled there for breeding to Manuel's stud dog, Tomas, was a fine looking bitch that belonged to the President of the Canary Dog Club of Gran Canaria.

However, to say that the Canary Dog, as a breed, is simply a composition of English Mastiffs, English Bulldogs, and whatever native breed might have been used is a fallacy. English breeds were undoubtedly used in the production of Canary Dogs, but many other European breeds have been used as well. The Neapolitan Mastiff, for example, clearly figures into Canary Dog breeding. So to a minor extent does the American Pit Bull Terrier figure into Canary Dog breeding on the island of Gran Canaria. But at least as important as the non-Spanish breeds that were used in the production of the Canary Dog are the Spanish breeds,

Leone, a Canary Dog from Naples, Italy, certainly appears to
be at least as much Neapolitan Mastiff as anything else. It's no
coincidence that he lives in Naples, the homeland of the Neo.
Manuel Curto does mention that the Neo has been used in some
Canary Dog breeding, and Leone seems living proof.

and the native Canarian breeds, that figure into Canary Dog
genealogy (such as the Majorero, a cattle-herding breed also
occasionally used for fighting, and the Bardino). Perhaps it
takes a trip to the Canaries to get a feel for this. Perhaps
one needs to see for himself how many local dogs are mixed
with Canary Dog, and how many Spanish breeds have been
intentionally crossed to Canary Dog, to appreciate and to
fully understand the complexity of Canary Dog genealogy.

This is a breed that has been created, and to some extent
is still being modified, with an end in mind, more than it is
a breed that is simply the product of a crossbreeding of a
handful of breeds. This is a breed that is being produced, some
might argue that it is still being composed, in order to satisfy

a number of demands. One demand is its appearance. In the United States we are accustomed to breeds that are produced for aesthetic reasons alone, or for functional reasons alone. The Canary Dog does not fit this mold well at all. Breeders of the Canary Dog do have aesthetics in mind as they are definitely trying to preserve something from the past. But they have function in mind as well. More complicated still is the fact that they have many functions in mind.

For one thing, and for those of you who have become bored by all the talk that has gone on so far, this is the time to put your thinking cap back on, the Canary Dog is being produced as a modern-day fighting dog. The Canary Dog is also being produced as a guard dog, and at this task the Canary Dog serves as admirably as any breed alive. Thirdly, let's remember the proper Spanish breed name. It is Perro de Presa Canario. Translated, this means Dog of Prey of the Canary Islands.

I asked Manuel Curto Gracia what the prey of this dog is or was. I knew the answer had to be hogs, but I also knew that there are no hogs on the islands. I'll tell you what there are on the islands. The people eat a wide variety of seafood. I finally came to understand what the difference is between really fresh seafood and seafood as we know it on the streets of NYC. Anyway, in addition to a wide variety of food from the sea, the people eat chicken. To appreciate the chicken, one must come to know a red sauce known as Mojo, that is a big part of island cuisine. It's great, for lovers of garlic. In addition to seafood and chicken, the people eat rabbit, and to this end, Manuel also raises Podenco Canario, a rabbit hunting breed that I recognized at his kennels, much to his surprise. And in addition to rabbit, chicken and seafood,

Dr. Fernando Melendez of San Diego, California provides us with these three historical photographs taken on the Canary island of Las Palmas. This is Dr. Melendez's father, Fernando as a boy, who grew up to be a distinguished Spanish Navy Admiral. The dogs depicted might be Great Danes as Dr. Melendez suspected, but the author is more inclined to believe, given the context of the photographs, that these dogs are the now extinct Spanish breed, Alano. There is currently a serious effort being made in Spain to reconstruct this breed, though the original population has long since disappeared. Research into the Alano leads the author to believe that the breed would have very much resembled a good working Great Dane. The photograph (*below*) shows Dr. Melendez's father and aunt, taken in Las Palmas circa 1903.

Canarian people eat goats. But they don't eat pigs. In fact, if you order barbecued ribs, thinking that you'll be getting a plate of pork ribs, you will be quite surprised to find that you will be served barbecued goat ribs.

But they don't eat pigs. Because pigs are not kept and are not eaten on the Canaries, I feel that my breed name "Canary Dog," as opposed to the proper breed name Perro de Presa Canario is even more useful than I thought it was before. This breed's ancestral component breeds may once have been a hog-catching dogs, but it is no longer a hog-catching dog. It is a guard dog, and it is a fighting dog, and it is from the Canary Islands, hence, as far as I am concerned, it is 'The Canary Dog." When I asked Manuel Curto about my name for this breed, he agreed that he would have no problem with it. If there is a potential problem with this breed name, it is only that people from the Canaries might view any dog from the islands as being a Canary Dog. From our perspective, however, this name is much easier to pronounce than Perro de Presa Canario is.

I said earlier that the Canary Dog is still being used as a fighting dog. To say that the Canary Dog is still being used as a fighting dog is to say a great deal about its form having to follow function. It also tells us a great deal about the general temperament of the breed. A number of people I spoke with in Tenerife assured me that the fighting was conducted on Gran Canaria, for the most part, as opposed to on Tenerife, but this is typical of what dog fighters will tell an outsider about who is doing the dog fighting. On Gran Canaria many Pit Bulls have been imported for use as fighting dogs, both against other Pit Bulls and against Canary Dogs. For the most part, Canary Dogs are not matched against Pit Bulls

Vega II de Curto, another of Manuel
Curto's brood bitches.

Note the difference between the two pups owned by Rudolf
Sewerin of Germany: the one with the white chest is a Presa
Mallorquin and the brindle pup is a Canary Dog (or Presa
Canario). The Mallorquin is a more recent reconstruction of an
extinct breed.

due to the unfair difference in size between these two breeds.
Canary Dogs are normally matched against Canary Dogs.
In some instances, three or four Canary Dogs are put in a
makeshift arena together to allow all hell to break loose and
to see which dog will walk out.

But in some instances Pit Bulls are matched against
Canary Dogs as well. To the credit of the dog fighters of
the Canary Islands, they do not simply proclaim that their
dogs are the best fighting dogs in the world, as so many
Americans do. When asked which is the better fighting

Jessy, a male Canary dog owned by
Sigi Aler.

breed, they offer the only answer that makes sense: they say
"Well, that depends upon the Pit Bull being used in the
match, and it depends upon the Canary Dog." As near as I
could determine, a Canary Dog can be very punishing, and a
good one can fight for 35 minutes. Pit Bulls that do well are
sometimes used in Canary Dog breeding, especially on the
island of Gran Canaria. Pit Bull admixture is not as common
on Tenerife.

Show Stopper Cassiopia, a 16-month
old Canary Dog bitch, weighing 95
pounds at 24 inches tall.

The Canary Dog is wonderfully suited for guard work. This is a very tough, low-keyed, suspicious, hard, loyal, obedient breed. All in all, I can tell you that a good Canary Dog, like Manuel Curto's Tomas, is one of the most impressive dogs on the face of the earth.

Manuel gave me a demonstration that many a Pit Bull breeder will find difficult to believe. I will tell you that I saw this demonstration with my own eyes. There is no question as to its validity. Manuel took me into one of his kennel buildings. All of his kennel buildings are made of cement, with both indoor and outdoor runs. A hallway runs through the middle of each building, with doors running against each wall. Even in the oppressive heat of the Canary Islands, the buildings are cool. He slides open a door, and he is in a run.

On this occasion, he took me to a run full of puppies that were about seven weeks old. Remember, these are Canary Dog pups and so, they are very large. These aren't Pit Bulls. None of these pups had ever been out of the run before. This

Jessy, owned by Sigi Aler.

was to be a demonstration of how these dogs "have no fear, and feel no pain." As soon as Manuel opened the door of the run, the litter of pups ran to us. There was no hesitation or trepidation. They came to us as if they knew us well. Then, as we were talking about one of the pups in particular, Manuel grabbed it by its tail and hoisted it up, five feet above the floor. Not only was there no whimper of pain, there was no change of expression on the puppy's face. It never turned around to see what had it by the tail.

Next, Manuel grabbed hold of its ear and held tight. He

Leone from Naples, Italy. Compare Leone's head to some of the heads from the kennel of Manuel Curto. How important it is to follow the guide of good dogs from the Canary Islands.

let go of the tail, and the pup dropped down, being kept from falling only by the hold on the ear. Again, there was not a whimper. There was no change of expression on the face of the pup. Again, it never turned its face to see what had it by the ear. Finally, Manuel put the puppy down. It quickly rejoined its littermates in jumping up on our shins in demand of attention. The experience did not affect the pup in the least.

I'll tell you what else I noticed about these dogs with regard to their lack of all reaction to rough handling. Manuel has the habit of thumping his adult dogs on the side, affectionately. Many of us do this to our dogs, but Manuel's thumps are comparatively attention getting. I watched him thump his dogs as he finished showing each individual to me and just before he would turn to return it to its run. He would give each a hard thump on the side. Never once did a dog react in

Mory de Irema Curto, a typical dark
brindle Canary Dog from Tenerife.

any way to the thump. In some dogs, one would detect a bit
of pain perhaps. In other dogs, the dog would turn toward
the thump to return the affection in some "doggy manner."
These dogs did absolutely nothing. They didn't cringe. They
didn't turn in response. They didn't change the expression
on their face. They simply did nothing at all and this struck
me as being unusual. I only began to understand this lack of
response when I saw the total lack of reaction on the part of
the puppy to being hoisted up by its tail and then by its ear.

The color of the Canary Dog is of great interest to me.
When I asked Manuel Curto what color should be selected
for the show ring, from among the dark brindles, the white
patched, lighter-coated brindles, and the fawns, many of

Left: Show Stopper Bad Mama Jamba, two-year-old bitch weighing 100 pounds at 22 inches tall. *Right:* Show Stopper Poseidon, six-month old dog weighing 80 pounds.

which sport black masks, he said there is to be no preference among these dogs, all other factors being equal. Yet, in his kennel, all but one bitch was a brindle dog. He mentioned that he, personally, preferred the color, but he gave no reason as to why. He showed me a dark brindle puppy that he liked the best.

I also prefer the brindle dogs, but I will not tell you that this is simply a matter of personal preference. I prefer them to the fawn-coated dogs because the brindling is what is found in so many of the native breeds, especially the aforementioned Majorero, a cattle-herding and sometimes fighting breed that factored heavily into the ancestry of the Presa Canario. For my money, the fawns remind me too much of the English breeds that figure into their ancestry. Many fawn-coated Canary Dogs have a very Bullmastiff-like appearance, and I think that this is to be avoided. My strong suggestion to those Americans who have and who

Left: Show Stopper Calybos, two-year-old dog weighing 135 pounds at 25.5. inches tall. *Right*: Show Stopper Andromyna, two-year-old bitch weighing 90 pounds at 22.5 inches.

will become interested in importing these dogs is to bring in the brindles for this reason.

I have always preferred owning a male dog, as opposed to a bitch, for no good reason. I have always felt that the male of a breed offers me more of everything I got interested in the breed for than the bitch does. But among Canary Dogs, my preference for males is particularly strong. Not only does the male offer a much more "macho" appearance, but the temperament seems much bolder among the males than the females. This is a preference I rarely feel strongly enough about to communicate to others. A black-masked fawn Canary Dog bitch is much too much like a Bullmastiff bitch in appearance for me.

I really think that the Canary Dog could have a strong, solid future among American purebred enthusiasts. It's a low-maintenance breed that while large, isn't as large as the Mastiff. It is more the size of the American Bulldog. It is

Four-year-old dog, Reba, weighing 100
pounds at 22 inches tall.

calm by nature and so will fit into a home more easily than
many of the breeds we commonly accept as pets already. It
is shorthaired, and while it is sturdy enough to tolerate cold
temperatures, the breed comes from an exceedingly hot place.
It is a very serious and able guardian breed, and the need for
such dogs grows in the States all the time. This is definitely
a manstopper.

Before leaving this chapter, I would like to comment
on some of the criticism I have heard of some of the first
Canary Dogs to find their way to the United States. The
primary criticism is that basically this is a large Pit Bull, and
we already have that. Folks, this is not a large Pit Bull. It
actually took seeing the dogs in their native environment
for me to fully appreciate some of the Canary Dogs I had
seen here before making my trip. This does not mean that

every would-be Canary Dog you will see in this country is a good representative of the breed either. Look at the pictures I've offered here. These are Canary Dogs. If what you come across here doesn't appeal to you as much as these dogs do, perhaps you need to keep looking as opposed to becoming discouraged with the breed. We will have the good dogs here in time, and when we do, it will have been worth the effort we expended to obtain them.

Well, so much for my trip to the Canary Islands. It was a fun trip, a memorable family vacation, and I spent a great day "dogging." I feel like I understand these dogs now and have developed an appreciation of them that may not have been as possible otherwise. It's funny, but when I left Manuel's kennel, I found myself thinking that it is a very curious human phenomenon that I could go to this strange and far off place to meet a man, who grew up so entirely differently than I did, who is nonetheless much more like myself than the men who live just next door to me. Such is life, I suppose.

Above left and below: Toni, owned by Stefan Baumgartner with agitator Dirk Schuett. Clearly intended for hard protection work, the Canary Dog means business. *Above right:* Jorge, owned by Siegfried Adelfinger of Germany, on the sleeve.

Above and below: Toni, coming toward the agitator and hitting him hard!

Above and below: Canary Dog owned by Dr. Rudolf Sewerin biting the sleeve. The agitator is Sigi Adelfinger. This breed is a serious and effective guard dog, and any working-dog enthusiast who is not impressed is making a big mistake.

Above and below: Dr. Rudolf Sewerin's dogs training hard.

SOUTH AFRICAN
BOERBOEL

I have tried to make the point in various places throughout this book that, in my opinion, in order to truly understand a breed of dog, one must first fully understand the place the breed originated, the dog's relationship to that place, the people who first produced and then maintained the breed in question, and the reason those people were and are interested in the breed. In no case is this more true than with the South African Boerboel. In order to understand the Boerboel, one must understand both the natural environment of South Africa and the cultural and political situations faced by the Afrikaner people both now and in the past.

Let's talk about the environmental situation first. During the course of writing this book I did some traveling. One of

Welleen Yster out of Walleen Shibas by Donkerhoer Boeliie, owned by M. Schickerling and was bred by J.D. Boerdery. He stands 25 inches tall and weighs 139 pounds. At first glance, this dog might look like a Bullmastiff, but it is a working dog indeed, and according to his owner has one leopard kill under his belt. I know. It's hard to believe.

the places I traveled to was South Africa. While in South Africa, I visited the area around Capetown, Franschhoek, Gordon's Bay, Paarl, etc., and I also visited the area north of "Jo Berg" known as the Transvaal, in and around Krueger National Park. When one thinks of "Africa" and "the bush" and the incredible African wildlife, it is primarily that area in and around Krueger that one has in mind. To give you an idea of what we are talking about here, bear in mind that Krueger is a totally undeveloped wildlife area left in its natural state so that the African wildlife we all dream of can continue to exist. Krueger is surrounded by "game preserves." These preserves are huge and undeveloped, for the most part, and there are no fences between these preserves and Krueger

Dave Darson with his three-month-old Boerboel pup, Bacchus,
whom he brought home with him after a trip to South Africa.
Dave was one of the first in the U.S. to own this rare South
African breed.

National Park. Just the park, without the preserve land, is
roughly the size of Belgium.

Animals abound in this area of South Africa and many
of these animals are dangerous to man. Cobras can be found
here as well as crocodiles, hippos, rhinos, water buffalo
(which many say are the single most dangerous animal in all
of Africa), lions, leopards, hyenas, etc. Any of these animals
will kill a man. Many will go out of their way to kill a man.
Some will actually hunt, kill and eat a man.

I found that as a novice to "bush life," I was a sitting duck,
so to speak, in Africa. In New York City, where I was born
and raised, I learned how to survive as I was growing up. My
antenna was and is always up. I have developed a sixth sense

Here's Bacchus, growing like a weed at
three months ofage, already weighing
48 pounds. His sire weighs 160 pounds
and resides in Capetown, South Africa.

for getting around the city safely. I know where I can go and
when I can go there. I know how to act when "a situation"
arises. As a result, to date, I have lived far into middle age
without ever having had "an incident" in the city.

I don't know this "stuff" about Africa. Contrarily, in the
eastern United States, when I am walking in the woods, as I
do very often, there is really nothing at all to fear. One might
come across a rattlesnake or a copperhead, or even a black
bear, but none of these animals want anything do with man
and they normally detect man's presence and take off before
man will even get a chance to see them. On rare occasions, I
have come across all of these animals without incident and,
as a result, I walk through the woods without fear. I took this

Piona Rampai out of Piona Leeza by Dopper Olbaas,
owned by Kobus Rust of South Africa, bred by Wena
and Abri Pio. He is 28 inches tall and weighs 143 pounds.
You can see at least as much Rhodesian Ridgeback
in this dog as you can Bullmastiff but any crossbreeding
goes way back.

general feeling of safety and of self confidence with me when
I visited Africa, and this naivete can be very serious and even
deadly in the bush.

The "locals" in the bush have grown up with the same
kind of "sixth sense" that I have, only where mine is adapted
to New York City life, theirs is adapted to the dangers of
the bush. When in the bush, they walk quietly. They keep
their ears open and their eyes open. They look for "sign,"

371

Nako Bianca out of Grasland Lady by
Maestro XXIII Bruno. She stands 25
inches and weighs 123 pounds. Owner,
Kobus Rust. Breeder, Koos Kruger.
Mr. Rust is the chairman of the Sud-
Afrikaanse Boerboel Telersvereniqinq
(SABT).

or indications that animals might be near. They listen for a warning grunt that a lion might let out if it is not hunting but does not appreciate the fact that you are passing too near. That grunt will precede an attack. They look for movement that might indicate that an elephant is occupying the path ahead. I did not have a healthy enough fear of the bush.

Piona Bas Bas and Egoli Delila at 12 weeks of age. Owner, Kobus Rust. Note the puppies' serious expressions.

I walked too quickly and without enough caution. I talked too much and too loudly. I wasn't used to it.

Fortunately, this caused me to become the victim of only one halfhearted charge on the part of a bull elephant that I should have seen long before he saw me. I didn't. I was lucky enough to be walking along the rim of a ravine after having just come from watching some hippos in the Sabi River and the elephants were on the bottom of and across the ravine. One charged, ears out and trumpeting his head off. I began to run, which was stupid because it often precipitates a more serious attack and because one who runs in the bush could well run into a lion. In this case, the elephant decided that as long as I was running anyway, there was no need to charge all the way up the side of that ravine, and he left me alone. I learned a good lesson then and from that point onward I walked through the bush much more quietly and much more carefully.

373

Pups out of Jan-Su Spook Bouwer by Viviera Basjan at 12 weeks of age. The breeder Kobus Rustis, a serious working-dog breeder, was adamant about wanting to keep these dogs out of the hands of dogfighters and show-dog exhibitors. The Boerboel, as it exists today, is a totally functional working dog.

But children can't necessarily be expected to live in the bush and always exercise the degree of caution that the bush demands, even if they are raised in the bush. Kids will be kids. Lions will be lions. Leopards, cheetah, etc., will also be what they are. While I spoke with many people who had managed to grow up safely in the bush, all had stories of very close calls with large and dangerous animals when they were growing up.

Understanding this about the bush, one can now appreciate the demands placed upon a dog that is kept for use in defending the children living deep in the African bush. One of these demands is that the dog kept by the Afrikaner farmers living in the Transvaal and elsewhere in South Africa be willing to defend its human family against anything that might attack it. This calls for a totally fearless dog, as the

Viviera Basjan out of Graswater Tosca
by Piona Vegter, bred by F.S. Viuier and
owned by Kobus Rust. At 23 inches and
127 pounds, it is considered to be too
small for the breed.

attack might well be coming from a lion, a leopard, or a hyena. It also calls for a dog that is a tough enough fighting dog to live in a fight against such an adversary long enough for its family to escape. But this also calls for a dog that will always be both loyal and passive around every member of the family, children included. The dog must be that courageous, that tough, that devoted, and that safe.

The people who developed the Boerboel and who have maintained this breed to this day were and are Afrikaners, who are descended primarily from Dutch Calvinists and German and French Huguenots who settled in South Africa about 1652.

Mizpah Yvonne by Mizpoh Slukerbossie
out of Mizpah Jenny, bred and owned
by L.V.D. Merwe.

These people came to homestead deep in the bush and they
needed a dog that would protect them and their families as
they lived their lives. These people established themselves and
they developed a culture different than any other in the world.
But as time wore on, the political situation in South Africa
has changed and the culture of the Afrikaner, as it existed
for all of these years, has become seriously threatened. The
world has boycotted them for living lives that were perceived
as being racist by outsiders. Black Africans, with the help of
the rest of the world, have demanded that the way of life of
the Afrikaner be changed, and these proposed changes have
presented a threat to the culture of the Afrikaner people.
In response to this threat, many Afrikaners have mounted
serious efforts to preserve the culture that is threatened

A working Boerboel farm dog, a very lean and athletic young male.

and one aspect of this culture worthy of preservation is the Boerboel dog. As you read about the Boerboel, and the efforts mounted to preserve it, it is important that you realize that this breed of dog is more than just "a dog" to those who keep it. It is a very real part of a way of life. It is a genuine "aspect of culture."

This breed is representative of the pioneer spirit that allowed these people to exist in the face of the adversity that the African bush presented and continues to present. This spirit of enthusiasm for the culture of South Africa's non-aboriginal, European stock people became abundantly apparent in dealing with the people I came to know as a result of my having done the research required to write this chapter. The most helpful person among them was one Malcolm Wren of Capetown who originally contacted me for reasons unrelated to the Boerboel breed. Though Malcolm is a dog man, to be sure, his breed is the Bull Terrier, which is very

Left: Piona Lugar out of SmitTessa by Piona Vegter, owned by Kobus Rust and bred by Abri and Wena Pion. He weighs 121 pound and stands 25 inches tall. *Right*: Note the difference in type among Boerboel dogs if you compare this dog, Maestro XV Lelik out of Mizpah Sputnik by Slanat Charka to Piona Rampai. Breeder, Kobus Rust. Owner, Dr. Johan Goosen. He is 24 inches tall and weighs 154 pounds.

popular in South Africa, and his knowledge of the Boerboel was very limited.

Malcolm is a working parent and a busy guy; but when I first began to question him about the Boerboel, he decided he'd do me a favor and try to answer a few questions about the breed. To make a long story short, it wasn't more than a week from the time that we had originally established contact with each other that he had become totally engrossed in learning about the Boerboel and in no time at all he was thanking me for having prompted him to do the tremendous amount of research that he was doing in order to learn as much as he could learn about this aspect of his country's culture. He was writing people, visiting people, and calling people all over South Africa. He was taking breeders out to dinner. He

Salina, a two-and-a-half-year-old bitch,
owned by P. Louw. The dam was
Groenfontein Anka and the sire, Mizpah
Lucas.

was faxing me daily from Capetown, South Africa, where
he lives, to my home in New York. He was taking pictures
and mailing them to New York without ever asking me for
anything but to accept the information he was providing
and to use it with discretion. The bulk of the information
presented in this chapter came to me from one source or
another via Malcolm Wren and the great enthusiasm he
demonstrated in obtaining it and in providing it, is typical of
the spirit and of the interest in the culture that brings us the
Boerboel today.

Anyway, I certainly hope that you didn't mind having
had to suffer through my experiences in Africa and my

Maestro IDouglas out of Mizpah Jenny
by Jan-Su Daantjie Donderbos, owned
by A.V. D. Veen and bred by Kobus
Rust. He stands 27 inches tall and
weighs 172 pounds.

perception of what these dogs mean to these people too much, but I do think it is necessary to have heard this if you are to understand the breed. As I have already said, if we are to understand a breed of dog, we must first understand the people who developed and maintained it, the job the dog was intended to do, and the place in which the dog was expected to do its job. Hopefully, I was able to provide you with some insight into why the Boerboel is what it is. Now lets see if I can describe what the Boerboel is.

The term Boerboel is not an easy one to translate into English. In fact, having asked a number of South Africans to translate it from Afrikaans for me, and having asked a number of Dutchmen to do the same, I still don't understand the translation. At best these people have told me that this is simply a term which doesn't translate well. I understand the first part. "Boer" means farmer and the Boerboel is most definitely a farmer's dog. So "Boel" means dog, right? Wrong. That would be "Boerhond," a name formerly applied to the ferocious farm dogs of less specific type kept in South Africa before a definite type emerged. Bulldog, maybe? Nope. It means "to have a lot of stuff." So literally, Boerboel means "Farmer." "Have a lot of stuff." I guess on some very uncertain level, this makes sense. It's a farmer's dog with a lot of stuff? (The Right Stuff?)

Maybe the name refers to the great size of this farmer's dog? It is occasionally referred to as the "Farmer's Mastiff." Anyway, I'll guess the latter. Boerboel, we'll decide, means the Farmer's Mastiff.

Probably the first dog brought to South Africa that was used to give rise to the genetic line of dogs that would ultimately become the Boerboel breed was the early Bulldog [Bulleribijter) brought to "the Cape" by Jan van Riebeeck in 1652. This dog was described as being large, strong and of Mastiff type, which leads me to wonder if it was not the "Bearenbytef" type of the time as opposed to the "Bulleribijter." The Bulleribijter was a smaller, more bulldog-type dog used for bull baiting, whereas the Bearenbijter was a larger, more Mastiff-type dog used in bear baiting. While it doesn't make much difference today whether van Riebeeck's dog was one or the other, it is interesting that one of the nicknames that has emerged for the Boerboel is "the South Africa Bulldog." It could be that this name goes back to that early dog but, one way or another, the South Africans I have

Maestro WLIV Htswari out of Mizpah Jenny by Mizpah Jimmy, owned by Kobus Rust, weighs 112 pounds and stands 25 inches. What an athletic animal for a dog of this size!

spoken to do not support the use of this nickname (common in Europe).

Those Europeans who followed van Riebeeck to the Cape brought other large, tough and fierce dogs with them for use as protection against whatever might cause trouble. Keep in mind what an utterly hostile environment this was to settle, especially at that time, and ask yourself what kind of dog you would bring if you were leaving your homeland to become one of the first settlers in the Africa of the middle 1600s. This is the kind of dog these people brought. They brought the biggest, toughest, strongest, hardiest (remember, there was no veterinarian available), most fearless yet most loyal dogs they could find, and they used all of these dogs for breeding to other very tough dogs to produce the farm dogs required for the settlers in South Africa. These are the dogs and this is the breeding line that, being isolated and being very selectively bred for strength, loyalty, and courage, gave rise to the type of dog, indeed the "breed" of dog, which was to become the Boerboel.

So the Boerboel, as photographs reveal, appears like a Bullmastiff, of sorts, but we should not confuse these dogs with the Bullmastiffs we know today or with the Bullmastiffs of the past. The Bullmastiff breed was not brought to South Africa until about 1928 when this distinct breed was imported to South Africa for use in guarding diamond mines. However, about 1820 British settlers did bring Bulldogs and Mastiffs to the Cape with them and these dogs were also crossed with the type of dog that had been emerging in South Africa all along. It is very likely, and in fact it is suggested by Boerboel purists today, that some of the especially valuable working Bullmastiffs brought to South Africa for use in guarding diamond mines were crossed into the well-established "Boerhond" lines that were already in existence. It is claimed that this was especially true during the late 1940s and early 1950s among the farmers of the Northeast Free State, North Natal, and in parts of Transvaal. I will speculate that the Rhodesian Ridgeback may also have been used in the general breeding of Boerhond/Boerboel dogs, and it is also speculated by others in South Africa that working Great Danes of the past and working St. Bernards of the past were also used in the breeding of farm dogs.

So, when one thinks of the Boerboel of today, this cultural history as well as this genetic history should be kept firmly in mind. As the general Boerhond dogs of South Africa are the genetic stock from which the Boerboel breed emerged in its distinct form, all of these farm/protection bull and mastiff breeds are the genetic stock which gave rise to today's Boerboel. This is not to say that the Boerboel should be viewed as a crossbred dog today any more than all of the other purebreds of the world today can be. It is a composite of other working breeds that, being isolated, gave rise to a distinct physical and temperamental type of dog over a very long period of time.

The fact that the Boerboel exists as an established breed today is due to a small group of South Africans who formed the South African Boerboel Breeder's Association (SABBA). It was in 1980 that the founding members of SABBA arranged to meet at a high school in the village of "Senekal" in the "Free State." The primary interest which motivated these people was Africana, their culture, and as they were all Boerboel breeders, and as they all viewed the Boerboel dog as an example of living Africana. They set as their goal the preservation of the Boerboel in a pure form. Those who composed this group were: Johan De Jager, sheep farmer and chairman of the South African Wool Board, the owner of the Boerboel stud dog, "Rustverwacht" from Utrecht in Natal; Dr. Andre du Toit from the Paarl, a wine farmer and chairman of the world famous KWV Winery; Lucas Van Der Merwe from Kroonstad, a game rancher and Safari operator, the owner of huge Boerboel dogs, Plestiek and Flenters; Johan Du Freez of Senekal, a civil engineer and builder of bridges came with his Friedenheim Boerboels, Leeuw, Duiwel, and Mosadi; Mrs. Owen Read from Warden, owner of her Boerboel stud Venterspad; and the Nel Family from the Eastern Free State, owners of the "Moormoel" dogs.

These were the people who first formed SABBA, and

thousands of kilometers were traveled in search of a large core of the most typical Boerboels. When any advertisement for Boerboel pups appeared anywhere, someone followed it up to inspect the dogs being produced and as the dogs were located, the society's membership grew. Some of these were: Leon Riekert of Pretoria with his stud dog Leonard, Babs Bosman from Douglas with her "Ravata" dogs; Ella Louw from Volksrust with "Waterval"; Steyn Opperman from Ficksburg with her Christina; Nic Van Der Linde from Standerton with his "Geelbos" Boerboel; Klaas Van Waveren from Pietersburg in the Transvaal with "Ysterberg"; and more. These are some of the names of the foundation dogs used to secure the purity of today's Boerboel stock.

A number of Boerboels have been exported from South Africa. In November, 1994 a dozen was shipped to The Netherlands. By late 1996, the first two Boerboels found their way to the United States, one going to New York and the other to California.

The membership of SABBA definitely seems interested in getting this breed established outside of its homeland, but they are extremely cautious about who will own the breed and in what light it will be presented. They announced, via Malcolm Wren, that they would have to meet before allowing me to present their information in my book, I understood what they were trying to do and waited for Malcolm's word. I'm glad I did. This is a breed that should be presented to the world and one that should come to the world with the dignity with which it is perceived in its homeland. So, let's talk about the Boerboel.

The Boerboel qualifies to be included in this book because its ability to defend its human family against dangerous wild animals is an essential trait of the breed. Some of the stories about famous battles between Boerboels I believe. Others I don't. The stories about Boerboels killing lions I have difficulty with, to be honest. But the stories about Boerboels killing leopards I can believe. There is even one story about a Boerboel that killed four leopards during its career, finally being killed itself in its fifth battle with a leopard.

I've seen leopards in the wild in the Transvaal. To say I believe the stories about Boerboels killing leopards is a mouthful. I personally saw a female leopard in a tree feeding on an adult impala that the leopard had hunted and killed. It had then climbed the tree carrying the entire dead impala in its mouth to a high branch so that it and its cub could eat in peace, undisturbed by the hyena that was waiting for something, either impala or leopard cub, to fall from the tree. A leopard is a powerful, fast killing machine and for a dog to fight one and win requires that the dog be a very special, very powerful, very brave fighting machine itself.

This is the Boerboel's purpose. It lives in a land occupied by animals which kill to live and which will kill people, especially children, who fall victim to them. The Boerboel is the defender of its people and of its children and therefore, it must be a steady dog around the family and around the livestock which belongs to the farm on which it is raised. This is not to say that should this breed ever become much better known outside of its homeland that a watchful eye should not always be kept on a dog that is to be raised with young children, mind you.

Never take your children's safety for granted around any dog, no matter how highly regarded the reputation of the breed may be.

However, in its homeland it is the job of this farmer's dog to go into the field with the children by day and to protect them from whatever danger may present itself. By night, it is the job of the dog to lay by the fire and warn of any danger that may come around, always ready to defend the people of the house and the animals of the farm with its life, if need be.

It is a territorial dog. It will bark in warning and it will attack when it has to. It will fight with strange animals and, given its size, this is something that everyone should consider before getting the idea to bring one home as a pet in a populated area. This is a breed that is not known for its good nature around strange dogs.

The following is the standard for the Boerboel of South Africa as put forth by the South African Boerboel Breeder's Association (SABBA).

THE STANDARD OF THE BOERBOEL

General Appearance:

The Boerboel is a big, strong and sturdy dog with powerful muscles. His movements should be agile and his body should be sturdier, heavier, and bigger than the Boxer, but shorter in the leg than the Great Dane. The dog should not measure less (at the shoulder) than 66 cm and the bitch not less than 61 cm.

Character:

The Boerboel must be good-natured, intelligent, with a steadfast, well-balanced character and loyal to his master, even if it means losing its own life. He must show good watchdog qualities from a very early age and must love all members of the family, especially the children.

The Head:

This is one of the most important features of the dog as the whole character of the dog is reflected in the head. The head must be big, strong and broad between the ears. The upper jaw must be strong and broad at the back, with only a slight narrowing to the front. The lower jaw must be broad with only a slight narrowing to the front and should not protrude in front of the top jaw. (Author's note: I am told that at present, up to a maximum of a 1 cm protrusion is allowed but again, this is in a worst-case scenario.) The lips must be loose and fleshy and the top lip flaps must not hang over too low or appear too coarse and thick. The nose must be black—not liver colored. The nose or bridge of the nose should not be too long—between 8-10 cm, measured from the tip of the nose to a straight line between the eyes, where the eyes start. The nose bone must be straight, with very little or no tilting up like the Boxer— and the nose no longer than a Great Dane. The head must definitely be a "Boel" head with a strong mouth which melts in symmetrically with the head. No teddybear look. The head of the bitch would naturally be slightly smaller and appear more feminine than the dog's. The ears must be floppy and of medium size and fit the head.

Build of Body:

The neck—strong and thick with sufficient length to go with the body, also strong and muscled with loose skin. The top of the neck should be straight and blend well into the shoulders.

The back—strong, broad and straight, slightly hunched over the haunches is acceptable.

The chest—broad and strong with the loose skin of the neck blending in and taut between the front legs, which should be widely spaced to accommodate the broad chest.

The legs—strong, straight and able to cany the body well with well-shaped paws.

The tail—preferably cut short.

The coat—short and smooth.

Color:

Brindle, yellow (lion), gray, tan, brown, with white markings, with or without black muzzles, will be acceptable. We are trying to achieve a single-color dog with no, or very little white. (Author's note: While some white is currently acceptable, it is to be discouraged.)

Eyes:

Light brown, yellow brown, and dark brown is acceptable. Blue or blue-gray is unacceptable.

CONCLUSION

When I wrote *The World of Fighting Dogs*, years ago, I did so because it was a book that I had looked for on the shelves of bookstores for a long time, and when I realized that I wasn't finding it because no one had written it, I decided that I would. When I finished the book, I felt that I would have no reason to ever write a book like that again.

After all, I said what I wanted to say. I categorized the fighting breeds, or the gladiator breeds, if you will, and I had long felt that they deserved to be categorized together, rather than scattered separately, into various groups, that had little or nothing to do with the history of these dogs. Sure, I felt that I could have said more than I did in each case, but that was a time for introduction, rather than for detailed

The Korean Jindo, captured on film by Hyungwon Kang.
Spectacular!

information. After all, many of the breeds I discussed in that book were unknown to American purebred enthusiasts. I felt that an introduction was all they would need to find themselves becoming popular, and in retrospect, I guess I was right.

Now that years have gone by since that book was published, the situation that each of these breeds finds itself in throughout the United States, and throughout the world, is completely different than it was years ago. In some instances I am glad for the change. In others, I feel that this breed, or that, has become too popular for its own good. But whether the change in status has had a positive or negative effect upon the breed in question, the change itself needed to be addressed and discussed openly.

Left: Boxer owned by Marianne Legere of California. This is Cherokee Oaks Panache, CGC. *Right*: Boerboel puppy at 12 weeks of age, bred by Kobus Rust.

As I sit here, I find myself again feeling that there will never be any need for me to write another book like this one. I've said all I want to say about dogs, and at this point I would find it to be more entertaining to read what someone else has to say instead. It might be fun to not write anymore at all, and to get out and do more instead. I have other interests too, and I would like to devote more of my time and more of my energy to them.

But who knows? Who knows where we will all be a decade from now? Maybe we will all be sitting right here, in the general condition we are in now. And maybe the dog scene will have changed so dramatically again that the new series of changes will demand discussion again! We'll see. Maybe we'll talk about the fighting dogs again. I can assure you that if I feel I have anything more to say on this subject, I will say it, thanks to you.

Bull Terrier at six years of age, owned
by Clive Mellor of Yorkshire, England.

But in any event, I'd like to reinforce that I have not written these books in order to stimulate some primal urge in young men to own dangerous dogs. I have tried to introduce you to some really fine companions that, when owned responsibly, will become a part of your life that you will recall with fond memories forever. I hope I have done that.

I have also tried to record a bit of human history. It sometimes bothers me that many live with the attitude that the best way to address the issue of dogfighting is not to address it at all. They feel the best thing to do when one opens the subject is to stop the discussion dead in its tracks, in the hope that this silence will somehow cause dogfighting to go away. It won't. People have bred fighting dogs throughout the world for a long, long time. People have bred these dogs

Two handsome Dogues de Bordeaux, Blue Blood Amos Reed
and his son Vesuvio Le Mugs.

before any of us were born, and they will undoubtedly breed
these dogs long after we are all gone. All I have done is to
observe this, and tell you what I have observed. Is that so
bad? I don't think so. I think that all of this discussion has
done little more than to give later generations something to
think about.

I realize that people are reading my books today too.
Has this encouraged anyone, anywhere, to do something
cruel and barbaric that he or she might not otherwise have
done? I feel confident that my books have not. People will do
what people will do. My books are not intended to instruct,
but rather to record that which is going on all around us.
I was trained as an anthropologist. Focusing on aspects of
culture which have not attracted much attention has always
interested me and these books are also an expression of that
interest.

I would like to leave you with this bit of advice. Own your
dogs responsibly. Learn to know when a dog is dangerous to

an innocent person and have the guts to do the right thing, no matter how difficult it may be, should you find that your dog is more man-aggressive than it should be. Keep in mind that you may own a dog for many years after you first bring it home. Your life may change a great deal in the time you will own the dog. Your living condition, may change dramatically too. Ask yourself before you take on the responsibility of dog ownership not only if you are in a position to own a dog like those discussed here but also if you will be in a position to care for it for all the years of its life. You'll be sorry if you make a mistake in this area, and so will I.

About the Author

CARL SEMENCIC was born in New York City and still lives within walking distance of the city line. He is the product of the NYC public education system and he holds a Associates Degree in Liberal Arts from Queensborough Community College, a B.A. in British and American Literature from Queens College, and a Master's Degree and Doctorate in anthropology from State University of New York at Stony Brook where his areas of special interest were the archaeology of the Americas and American Indian studies. He also holds an Advanced Certificate which he received "With Distinction" from the Wine and Spirit Education Trust and he has been employed in the fine wine industry since 1982. He's known to have a seriously educated wine palate.

Semencic is best known for his magazine articles and books about rare breeds of dogs. He wrote three of books using his own name and two more using false names when the mail became impossible for him to deal with. Many of the breeds he wrote about were on the verge of extinction when he began to popularize them in his writing.

Dr. Semencic is a life member of the National Rifle Association and an avid outdoorsman. He enjoys fishing, especially fresh water with ultra-lite equipment, hunting, but only with traditional muzzleloaders, kayaking, especially in the Great Okefenokee Swamp but also locally, and hiking. He has traveled the world both on business and for pleasure. He is also a member of the American Mensa Society.

Semencic distrusts government and describes himself as a Conservative, "closed-borders" Libertarian. He's been married to the same woman since 1979 and they have raised two sons to adulthood.

Of all the places he's been, he says that perhaps his all time favorite place is his own backyard. Either there or Queenstown, New Zealand.

ALSO AVAILABLE
BY DR. CARL SEMENCIC

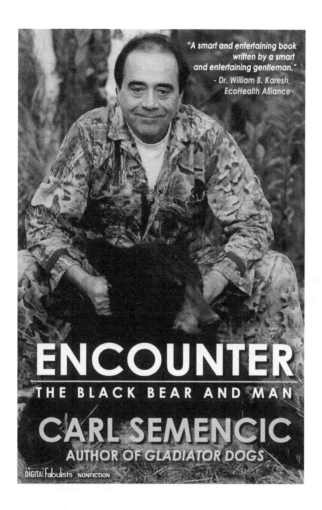

ENCOUNTER
THE BLACK BEAR AND MAN
CARL SEMENCIC
AUTHOR OF *GLADIATOR DOGS*
DIGITAL Fabulists NONFICTION

DIGITAL Fabulists

Printed in Poland
by Amazon Fulfillment
Poland Sp. z o.o., Wrocław

31188028R00244